Releasing the Prophetic

Releasing the Prophetic

Ryan LeStrange

ISBN: 1511864702
ISBN 13: 9781511864701

Contents

Foreword

Moses once said, "I wish that all the Lord's people were prophets and that the Lord would put His Spirit on them" (Num. 11:29). Although Paul pointed out in his first epistle to the church at Corinth that all are not prophets, all believers have a prophetic spirit because the Holy Spirit lives on the inside of them. And Joel prophesied that in the last days God would pour out His Spirit upon all people and that they would prophesy (Acts 2:17).

Prophetic ministry is absolutely critical in this hour—perhaps more critical than at any time in the history of the world. All believers need to develop the prophetic spirit that dwells on the inside of them. That process starts with understanding the gift of prophecy, which essentially edifies, exhorts and comforts (1 Cor. 14:3). It continues with learning how to steward and judge the gift of prophecy rightly and how to interpret and apply dreams and visions from the Lord.

The prophetic movement was birthed in the 1980s and we have come a long way toward understanding prophets and personal prophecy since the pioneering days of Bill Hamon and Cindy Jacobs. But there is still a lot of confusion about what prophets do, prophetic protocols and developing a prophetic culture in churches. Indeed, some still reject the role of the prophet and shun prophetic intercessors. Others depend too much on those with prophetic giftings because they have not been trained to incline their ear to the Lord. It is clear that we need more teaching and training in this vital ministry.

Ryan LeStrange is a trusted voice in the prophetic ministry. With a blend of revelation, practical insight and apostolic strategies, Ryan is giving a healthy expression to prophetic release in his traveling ministry. He is raising up prophetic sons and daughters in his local revival center. He is penning materials like this book, *Releasing the Prophetic*, that are inspiring many to press into their prophetic call in these last days.

There are many books on the prophetic. I have written a number of them myself. This book offers another piece to the prophetic puzzle, offering an apostolic perspective that is refreshing, teaching that is clear and inspiration that will bring identity to many.

In *Releasing the Prophetic*, you will hear from a man of God who understands all too well the problems in the modern-day prophetic movement but nevertheless is contending to see a generation of prophetic people rise up with an accurate voice that blows the trumpet, sounds the alarm, stands in the gap and otherwise follows the Holy Spirit as He leads and guides them into all truth.

As you turn the pages of this book, you will discover a boldness that stirs your spirit and a compassion that warms your soul. Whether you are brand new to prophetic ministry or a seasoned veteran, *Releasing the Prophetic* will make you hungrier to hear God's voice and give you guidelines for releasing a pure word of the Lord.

> Jennifer LeClaire
> Senior Editor, Charisma Magazine
> Director, Awakening House of Prayer
> Author, The Making of a Prophet

Endorsements

When I first preached for Pastor Ryan at Impact International Church I knew I was in a place where the people had been well taught concerning the things of the Spirit. And I believe Ryan's common sense approach concerning prophecy and the believer will enrich and strengthen your life and your relationship with the Lord.

Richard Roberts
Chariman and CEO
Oral Roberts Evangelistic Association

Apostle Paul stated that there were people in his time that had zeal with no knowledge. Guess what...? We have them too. One of the most needful areas where solid knowledge is needed today is in the area of the Prophetic Ministry. Dr. Ryan LeStrange has authored a timely book called **Releasing the Prophetic**. This exciting book gives the reader the needful insight to walk and relate to the prophetic ministry in a healthy and biblical manner. I recommend this book to all who want to enjoy the prophetic and avoid the pathetic that some call the prophetic ministry.

Roberts Liardon
Author of Best-selling Series:
God's Generals
Sarasota, Florida

The prophetic is multi-dimensional and has many flavors and expressions. Ryan does an excellent job of providing that multi-angled view of this powerful gift while anchoring each illustration from scripture. You'll enjoy the overall teaching and the many nuggets of truth that challenge your thought processes to think deeper about the impact of the prophetic ministry.

Jennifer Eivaz, Pastor
Author of The Intercessors Handbook

Introduction

The **Prophetic Ministry** is perhaps one of the most misunderstood ministries in the modern Church. Many Pastors have had negative experiences with prophetic people who had an abundance of zeal but lacked proper training and development. Many believers have attended Charismatic meetings and received words from people whom they did not know which brought more confusion than clarity.

In this fast-moving, information-saturated world in which we live, the Church is progressing, evolving and adapting. I believe that Paul and the Apostles of the Bible would have employed technology to reach the masses, teach the believers and release God's awesome power to the world, still much of the leadership of the modern Church has moved in the opposite direction. Many churches that believe in being Spirit-filled and embrace the full gospel message may teach and talk about it but leave little to no room for the moving of the Holy Spirit.

We live in a world that was created by a **Supernatural,** all-knowing, all-powerful God! We are continually reminded of the supernatural as Hollywood releases an increasing number of productions about ghosts, witches, vampires and the after-life. Yet, the Church has decided to take a turn toward hu-man understanding, predictability and production rather than the supernatural. What is the logic? Many church leaders are adamant that people simply do not want the supernatural, that they are afraid of any type of expression of God that is "outside of the box." When did we get permission to put the King of the Universe in the box? What kind of sense does it make to preach from a book that we claim was **Supernaturally** written, inspired and produced while rejecting the supernatural ministry of Jesus in today's world? This is nothing more than anti-Christ spirits choking the life of God out of the people of God! Our culture is embracing the supernatural on television, in movies and entertainment but the Church world is locking the Holy Spirit out!

I believe that there is a growing hunger inside of God's peo-ple for authentic Spirit-led ministry that embraces the Power of the Holy Spirit. Many people are tired of filing into a church full of people yet void of God's presence. Predictable gatherings and watered-down sermons have fueled a growing void in the hearts of people who were created to **know** and experience the most powerful and amazing person in history, Jesus.

Trapped inside of dry churches are many prophetic peo-ple who feel stuck, weary and complacent. The truth is that the prophetic ministry is one of the most powerful and life-giving ministries in the Body of Christ. There is nothing like a clear and concise word given to a person who is strug-gling. A single prophetic word can often peel away layers of discouragement.

One of the arguments against the prophetic ministry is that it may get messy. I don't think that the mighty revival we read about in the book of Acts was sanitized and without controversy. When the prophetic ministry is properly taught, established and recognized in the Church it becomes a valuable tool releasing insight, direction, strength and encouragement.

And Elisha said unto him, Take bow and arrows. And he took unto him bow and arrows. And he said to the king of Israel, Put thine hand upon the bow. And he put his hand upon it: and Elisha put his hands upon the king's hands. And he said, Open the window eastward. And he opened it. Then Elisha said, Shoot. And he shot. And he said, The arrow of the Lord's deliverance, and the arrow of deliverance from Syria: for thou shalt smite the Syrians in Aphek, till thou have consumed them. (2 Kings 13:15-17)

Elisha released a prophetic word to the king to take the arrows, shoot strategically and then the arrows of the Lord's deliverance would set them free. The word of the Lord provided direction to the king. Prophetic words give much needed insight and release divine instructions.

The prophetic ministry is often the tip of the arrow that cuts through the assignments of the enemy and releases powerful freedom. Prophets by nature are spiritual warriors, who expose the hidden plots of the enemy. One of the greatest tools of Satan is deception. He attacks people and conceals the truth from them in order to keep them bound. The prophetic ministry brings the light of God and shines it upon hidden lies and schemes of the devil.

This charge I commit unto thee, son Timothy, according to the prophecies which went before on thee, that thou by them mightest war a good warfare. (1Timothy 1:18)

Prophetic words fuel faith and empower spiritual warfare. When a believer takes on a prophetic identity and begins to be led by the Holy Spirit they are equipped to combat the enemy. God warns us of coming attacks before they arrive! When a church takes on a prophetic spirit the enemy has a much more difficult time penetrating the body and getting a foothold because the people are in tune with what is happening in the spirit realm.

Not everyone who receives revelation from the Lord or gives a prophetic word will walk in the office of a Prophet. It is possible for much confusion to enter the prophetic ministry when believers receive prophetic impartation and equipping. As they begin to see things on another level, they oftentimes assume that they are being called to the Prophet's office. This is one of the many challenges that arise when we establish prophetic ministry in the Body of Christ. With proper training and understanding people can be taught beyond this wrong thinking. Any gift or ministry has challenges but the question becomes, "Is the fruit outweighing the small struggles along the way?" Concerning prophetic ministry, I say wholeheartedly, "Yes!"

CHAPTER 1

Why is The Prophetic Ministry Important?

A s with any ministry that God has given to the Church there are vital dimensions of the prophetic ministry that have the potential to shift the course of life in nations, regions, churches, ministries and individuals. Throughout history God has used Prophets to reveal His heart, fuel the passion of intimacy with God and warn His people of impending crisis.

The prophetic ministry brings a powerful sensitivity to the people of God. When you cut off the Prophets, prophetic messages and ministry, you create an atmosphere that is driven primarily by intellect and understanding more than life-changing revelation. Developing our intellectual capabilities is important but accessing God's promises, provisions and miracles is not something which can be accomplished by the mind alone but by the inner man.

An atmosphere that lacks prophetic direction typically becomes dry and stale. When a church rejects the prophetic ministry they embrace a culture that is driven much more by natural wisdom than spiritual power.

Some of the words associated with the prophetic are: **revelation, insight, leading, knowing, seeing, speaking, declaring, establishing, building, rooting out, exposing and tearing down.** The life of a Christian **must** be one that is led by the Holy Spirit. It is absolutely impossible to navigate our assignment on earth properly and advance the Kingdom without insight and revelation from God! Our born-again spirit was created by the Father as a place of illumination and understanding.

> **The spirit of man is the candle of the Lord, searching all the inward parts of the belly. (Proverbs 20:27)**

When we became born-again we were reconciled with God! Every wall was torn down and we were given free access to the Father:

> **And all things are of God, who hath reconciled us to himself by Jesus Christ, and hath given to us the ministry of reconciliation; To wit, that God was in Christ, reconciling the world unto himself, not imputing their trespasses unto them; and hath committed unto us the word of reconciliation. (2 Corinthians 5:18-19)**

> **But now in Christ Jesus ye who sometimes were far off are made nigh by the blood of Christ. For he is our peace, who hath made both one, and hath**

broken down the middle wall of partition between us. (Ephesians 2:13-14)

Who hath delivered us from the power of darkness, and hath translated us into the kingdom of his dear Son: In whom we have redemption through his blood, even the forgiveness of sins. (Colossians 1:13-14)

All of these verses demonstrate that Jesus did a complete work at Calvary! He paid the price and **fully redeemed** us. The enemy has absolutely no right to a blood-bought child of God. In the process of salvation, our spirit man was remade into the very image and likeness of God. This means that we are not earthly people who occasionally taste, touch and sense the heavenly realm. We are actually spirit people who happen to be living on earth for a season with the purpose of manifesting the Kingdom of God!

Experiencing supernatural things should be totally natural for us as believers. We should be hearing the voice of God on a frequent basis. It is the lies and accusations of the enemy which attempt to hold us back from walking in all that Jesus bought for us!

And I heard a loud voice saying in heaven, Now is come salvation, and strength, and the kingdom of our God, and the power of his Christ: for the accuser of our brethren is cast down, which accused them before our God day and night. (Revelation 12:10)

Satan is the accuser of the brethren. He continually brings false accusation against the people of God to get them to live beneath their birthright! Despite the fact that your born-again spirit man is hardwired to hear from heaven, the enemy will work overtime to convince you that you cannot hear God. It is your birthright as a child of God to be led by the Spirit of God.

And are built upon the foundation of the apostles and prophets, Jesus Christ himself being the chief corner stone. (Ephesians 2:20)

The prophetic anointing is foundational and partners with the apostolic in order to advance the Kingdom. The Prophet assists the Apostle by providing the building word of the Lord. The prophetic voice decrees the precise word for the region and the people while the Apostle governs the word and the work. When these two gifts work side-by-side there is an explosive effect that tears down long-standing religious barriers and brings forth immeasurable Kingdom results!

Rulers are typically partnered with prophetic voices. In Second Samuel and First Kings, we find that God sent the Prophet Nathan to King David. Nathan advised King David concerning his desire to build the temple of the Lord. It was he who confronted the king and led him to repentance after his sin with Bathsheba. Nathan also assisted in making Solomon the next king. The prophetic ministry of Nathan was vital in David's rule as king.

Rulership is an attribute of the apostolic anointing. Apostles are given a governing authority to establish Kingdom influence in a territory or people. They are sent with a heavenly mandate to bring transformation and change the spiritual climate.

But we will not boast of things without our measure, but according to the measure of the rule which God hath distributed to us, a measure to reach even unto you. (2 Corinthians 10:13)

Apostles are given a specific measure of influence based upon their particular assignment. The Apostle Paul was the spiritual father of the Corinthian church and counted them among his sphere of apostolic authority and rule.

And the Spirit of the Lord will come upon thee, and thou shalt prophesy with them, and shalt be turned into another man. And let it be, when these signs are come unto thee, that thou do as occasion serve thee; for God is with thee. And thou shalt go down before me to Gilgal; and, behold, I will come down unto thee, to offer burnt offerings, and to sacrifice sacrifices of peace offerings: seven days shalt thou tarry, till I come to thee, and shew thee what thou shalt do. And it was so, that when he had turned his back to go from Samuel, God gave him another heart: and all those signs came to pass that day. And when they came thither to the hill, behold, a company of prophets met him; and the Spirit of God came upon him, and he prophesied among them. (1 Samuel 10:6-10)

One function of the prophetic gift is to speak to kings. The prophetic anointing provides spiritual insight to the kingly (rulership) anointing. In today's Church this should be two-fold:

1. Prophetic anointing partnering with the apostolic kingly anointing providing spiritual wisdom and insight.

2. Prophetic anointing partnering with kingly financial anointing: speaking into the lives of the "kings" who are called to fund the work of God. There are many kings who have not risen to their appointed place of influence because they have been cut off from the prophetic voice.

Prophets are **Forerunners.** This is one reason why they get along so well with Apostles. Both of these gifts are out pioneering. They are like God's weapons out on the frontlines, tearing down the structures and plans of darkness, building the Kingdom of God. Prophets are visionary people who see and move in an advanced stage. Many times they are misunderstood because they are speaking something long before others are coming into the revelation. This is a vital part of their ministry gifting.

Nothing is created in the spirit realm without words. Prophetic words are filled with power, light *(divine illumination)* and creativity. Prophets declare what is coming in order to make way for its entry! They speak from the realm of the Spirit and release building words that Apostles can partner with to advance.

> **And he shall <u>go before</u> him in the spirit and power of Elias, to turn the hearts of the fathers to the children, and the disobedient to the wisdom of the just; to make ready a people prepared for the Lord. (Luke 1:17)**

The prophetic anointing was active and alive in the early Church and served as a powerful partner with the apostolic:

> **Then departed Barnabas to Tarsus, for to seek Saul: And when he had found him, he brought him unto Antioch. And it came to pass, that a whole year**

they assembled themselves with the church, and taught much people. And the disciples were called Christians first in Antioch. And in these days came prophets from Jerusalem unto Antioch. And there stood up one of them named Agabus, and signi-fied by the Spirit that there should be great dearth throughout all the world: which came to pass in the days of Claudius Caesar. Then the disciples, every man according to his ability, determined to send re-lief unto the brethren which dwelt in Judaea: Which also they did, and sent it to the elders by the hands of Barnabas and Saul. (Acts 11:25-30)

One key purpose of the prophetic ministry is to peel away the scales from the eyes of humanity, beginning with the Church.

He hath blinded their eyes, and hardened their heart; that they should not see with their eyes, nor understand with their heart, and be converted, and I should heal them. (John 12:40)

Therefore speak I to them in parables: because they seeing see not; and hearing they hear not, neither do they understand. And in them is fulfilled the prophecy of Esaias, which saith, By hearing ye shall hear, and shall not understand; and seeing ye shall see, and shall not perceive: For this people's heart is waxed gross, and their ears are dull of hearing, and their eyes they have closed; lest at any time they should see with their eyes, and hear with their ears, and should understand with their heart, and should be converted, and I should heal them. But blessed are your eyes, for they see: and your ears, for they hear. (Matthew 13:13-16)

7

When New Testament prophetic ministry is functioning, the word of the Lord speaks to the hearts of God's people and releases heaven's perspective into their lives. A person can be running from God when a prophetic word will pierce their heart as the Father reveals His heart to that person. Prophets and prophetic believers become mouthpieces for the Father as He leads them to share heavenly words and vision with people.

> **But if all prophesy, and there come in one that believeth not, or one unlearned, he is convinced of all, he is judged of all: And thus are the secrets of his heart made manifest; and so falling down on his face he will worship God, and report that God is in you of a truth. (1 Corinthians 14:24-25)**

As Paul was writing to the Corinthian church, providing wisdom, instructions and guidelines for prophetic ministry, he makes a profound statement. In these verses he is revealing the evangelistic potential of prophetic ministry. Paul states that when prophetic ministry is flowing and is authentic in a church, an unbeliever can come to receive a true word from God that reveals his heart's secrets. Then that prophecy draws him to the Father. Not only is this true in meetings but also outside of the Church!

As people become more hungry for the supernatural, they are turning to every sort of **false spirit** looking for power and insight. God clearly forbids the Church from engaging in any spiritual practice that is not biblical.

> *Regard not them that have familiar spirits, neither seek after wizards, to be defiled by them: I am the Lord your God. (Leviticus 19:31)*

> *There shall not be found among you any one that maketh his son or his daughter to pass through the fire, or that useth divination, or an observer of times, or an enchanter, or a witch, Or a charmer, or a consulter with familiar spirits, or a wizard, or a necromancer. For all that do these things are an abomination unto the Lord: and because of these abominations the Lord thy God doth drive them out from before thee. (Deuteronomy 18:10-12)*

The Lord is very clear that a Christian should not be associating with false fire and witchcraft. In fact, participating in these things will provide an open door for demonic powers to influence your life and bring torment.

I once worked with a lady who had simply played with a Ouija board when she was a young lady but continued to face extreme torment and devilish manifestations throughout her adulthood. She eventually broke all ties, closed the doors and got free. We even had to pray over her house and take authority over every spirit that was visiting her property.

> *And many that believed came, and confessed, and shewed their deeds. Many of them also which used curious arts brought their books together, and burned them before all men: and they counted the*

price of them, and found it fifty thousand pieces of silver. So mightily grew the word of God and prevailed. (Acts 18:18-20)

Paul was leading a major revival with one of the fruits being people repenting of witchcraft and familiar spirits! They burned their books and all items associated with false spirits.

People who long for the supernatural can easily be led astray if they do not come to know Jesus and understand His word. One of the major problems in today's Church culture is the severe lack of supernatural ministry in many churches, particularly in the western world. However, the prophetic ministry can reach a person right where they are and bring them into a life-altering encounter with God. Not only can prophetic ministry reach someone inside of a church meeting but also on the job, in the marketplace or on the streets.

The prophetic ministry is a power twin with the evangelistic ministry. There is a radical generation of prophetic people arising who are willing to go outside of the Church and be a voice for the Lord. God is using prophetic evangelism in an explosive way! What would happen in the cities of the nations if the Church really got hold of the prophetic anointing and people began to reveal the contents of men's hearts all over the city, releasing healing, restoration and freedom? I believe entire regions would be shaken with multitudes coming to Jesus. This is possible if the prophetic ministry is understood, taught and properly activated.

One of the primary opponents of genuine prophetic ministry is the religious spirit. At the heart of religion is a spirit of slavery that traps a person in a cycle of dead works and causes them to miss the reality of the Living Christ. People bound with a religious spirit walk under a heavy banner of condemnation. They serve God from a position of guilt and unworthiness thereby missing the beautiful gift of grace and righteousness by faith.

The religious spirit fights vehemently to control, contain and hinder the move of God in the Body of Christ. Churches that become bound with the religious spirit have all types of nice social activities, excellently produced entrainment events and meticulously-planned, painfully predictable services. Understandably, there is no move of God! The religious spirit functions strongest in an old wineskin that is dry and operates under a paradigm of ministry that cannot contain the new wine.

Having a form of godliness, but denying the power thereof. (2 Timothy 3:5)

The primary aim of the religious spirit is to trap the believer in religious activity with no power, anointing or authority! The anointing of the Holy Spirit sets people free.

And it shall come to pass in that day, that his burden shall be taken away from off thy shoulder, and his yoke from off thy neck, and the yoke shall be destroyed because of the anointing. (Isaiah 10:27)

A religious spirit will not tolerate a flow of power and anointing. When the prophetic ministry is functioning at its highest level, there is continual insight and revelation that releases a powerful flow of God's Spirit and destroys the yoke of bondage. Religious spirits fight to keep people bound! They hide behind traditions, comfort and familiar thoughts with attitudes and sayings that have no basis in the word of God but have generally become accepted in religious circles.

The Prophet comes in and challenges the religious mindset and beckons people to become radically free to walk with God on another level. A true Prophet will quickly discern and challenge a religious spirit. This is one reason why there is a strong level of spiritual warfare around the prophetic ministry.

The prophetic anointing increases the spiritual sensitivity of the Church. As believers receive ministry, prophetic impartation, instruction and equipping from the Prophets, their spiritual eyes begin to see on a greater level.

> **Wherefore I also, after I heard of your faith in the Lord Jesus, and love unto all the saints, Cease not to give thanks for you, making mention of you in my prayers; That the God of our Lord Jesus Christ, the Father of glory, may give unto you the spirit of wisdom and revelation in the knowledge of him: The eyes of your understanding being enlightened; that ye may know what is the hope of his calling, and what the riches of the glory of his inheritance in the saints, And what is the exceeding greatness of his power to us-ward who believe, according to the working of his mighty power. (Ephesians 1:15-19)**

The prayer of the Apostle Paul for the Church was that God would open the eyes of our understanding or the eyes of the inner man. He was praying that the believers would live with spirit eyes wide open, receiving vision, direction and spiritual guidance! Every person has inner eyes of the Spirit that can see into the realm of the Spirit. There is clear guidance here. A major part of the development process of a prophetic person is to concentrate on living with spirit eyes open.

CHAPTER 2

Developing a Prophetic Spirit

As a believer you were never intended to walk in the dark without the light of revelation. Your life was created to be God's canvas upon which He paints a blessed and purposeful story. In order to develop a prophetic spirit in your own life, you must first demystify the concept.

It should be neither strange nor uncommon for a believer who sees into the spirit realm on some level to live out of Spirit leading rather than simple human thought. It is the lies of the religious spirit that have caused people to believe that their spiritual lives should be void of power and supernatural leading.

Now faith is the substance of things hoped for, the evidence of things not seen. (Hebrews 11:1)

Faith sees into the realm of the spirit. It looks far beyond the natural realm as perceived by the human senses, literally sees into the unseen realm and then boldly declares what has been seen. Faith is simply a spirit of seeing and saying.

The confession or proclamation of faith is one that is made as the inner eyes see into the spirit and are established upon truth. Unshakable faith is that which refuses to bow to the natural realm, choosing instead to hold fast to the promises of God. Faith is never birthed without insight!

The hearing ear, and the seeing eye, the Lord hath made even both of them. (Proverbs 20:12)

Our born-again spirit man is created to move in the spirit realm. We are called to be spirit beings temporarily living in a natural realm and continually manifesting the realm of the spirit. This is only possible by having spirit ears and eyes wide open!

And when the servant of the man of God was risen early, and gone forth, behold, an host compassed the city both with horses and chariots. And his servant said unto him, Alas, my master! how shall we do? And he answered, Fear not: for they that be with us are more than they that be with them. And Elisha prayed, and said, Lord, I pray thee, open his eyes, that he may see. And the Lord opened the eyes of the young man; and he saw: and, behold, the mountain was full of horses and chariots of fire round about Elisha. (2 Kings 6:15-17)

There was a mighty angel army ready to defend the people of God. They were there but unseen to the natural eye. Only when Elijah opened the spiritual eyes of his servant did he see the angelic host. There is another dimension around us all the time. This seems so mysterious but it actually isn't.

The reason that we are not more aware of the spirit realm is because we do not spend enough time tuning in. The access was granted by the free gift of salvation. When a person gets born-again, they are not only saved from a burning hell but they are made new! They are no longer born of flesh but of Spirit. So why would we not talk in the Spirit on a consistent basis?

One of the first steps is renewing your mind *(Romans 12:2)*. Get the word of God out and begin to study about your new nature and being led by the Spirit. As you place the truth in your mind you will begin to open up and receive.

Ask, and it shall be given you; seek, and ye shall find; knock, and it shall be opened unto you: For every one that asketh receiveth; and he that seeketh findeth; and to him that knocketh it shall be opened. (Matthew 7:7-8)

Seek Holy Spirit direction. Begin to thank God with your mouth for the leading of the Holy Spirit in your life. Claim the nine gifts of the Spirit. When I first learned that all the gifts were available to me as a believer, I began to name each one in my prayer time and claim their operation as God wills. I would lay hands upon my belly and call forth the rivers. Faith must be alive and active in order to receive its reward! Be bold in your faith. Go after the insight that belongs to you.

Spend quality time praying in the Spirit. This is an absolute master key. When you pray in other tongues to edify *(build up)* yourself, you are entering into the spirit realm and bypassing your mind. You are no longer communicating with other people but you are speaking with the tongues of angels.

Though I speak with the <u>tongues</u> of men and of <u>angels</u>, and have not charity, I am become as sounding brass, or a tinkling cymbal. (1 Corinthians 13:1)

Praying in other tongues is very different from worship. Worship can lift your soul *(mind, will and emotions)* up into the presence of God. Your mind can be overcome with emotion at times in deep worship. In the presence of God mental anguish is wiped away. When we sing songs in an earthly language our mind engages in the sentiment that is expressed and it becomes a glorious approach to the throne of God. When you pray in the Spirit your mind does not understand and there is no engagement of your soul.

For he that speaketh in an unknown tongue speaketh not unto men, but unto God: for no man understandeth him; howbeit in the spirit he speaketh mysteries. (1 Corinthians 14:2)

For if I pray in an unknown tongue, my spirit prayeth, but my understanding is unfruitful. What is it then? I will pray with the spirit, and I will pray with the understanding also: I will sing with the spirit, and I will sing with the understanding also. (1 Corinthians 14:14-15)

Praying in the Spirit bypasses the limitations of the human mind and prays the absolutely perfect will of God.

Likewise the Spirit also helpeth our infirmities: for we know not what we should pray for as we ought: but the Spirit itself maketh intercession for us with groanings which cannot be uttered. And he that searcheth the hearts knoweth what is the mind of

the Spirit, because he maketh intercession for the saints according to the will of God. (Romans 8:26-27)

As you pray in the Spirit, you are partnering with the person of the Holy Spirit to release God's plans and purposes for your life. When you pray for long periods of time, your mind may wander off because it is not being employed in the prayer. Your spirit is doing all the praying. Do not allow your mind to distract you.

I have found that as I pray in the Spirit, I often receive heavenly downloads. They do not always come immediately because the natural mind is much slower than the spirit mind! I have been driving down the road days later and all of a sudden like a flash of lightening across my mind, something is supernaturally illuminated to me. This is the result of spending time in the Spirit.

The Lord told his servant Habakkuk to write down what he saw (Habakkuk 2:2). As you spend time with God, listening and getting quiet before Him, expect Him to speak! Take something with you into your prayer time to write, record or type what He speaks to you. Before you are ever prophetic concerning anyone else's life, you must be prophetic in your own life. Prayer journaling and recording the word of the Lord from your time with Him is critical in the development of a prophetic spirit in your life.

Begin to recognize how God speaks:

Places Where God Talks to You

1. **Spiritual Mind**- Your spirit man has a mind. God speaks to your spirit mind in various ways.

And he that searcheth the hearts knoweth what is the mind of the Spirit, because he maketh intercession for the saints according to the will of God. (Romans 8:27)

Leadings that come through the mind of the Spirit:

- God thoughts- illuminations that come like thoughts but are born of the Spirit.
- Impressions- almost like a feeling; however, it is not mental but spiritual. You have an impression about something or someone and you know that it is deeper than a thought.
- Inward knowing- you just know something by the Spirit and there is no escaping it. It is not something that came to you through a tremendous encounter but just a simple knowing.
- Leading- the desire and prompting to move in a particular direction.
- Prompting- an unction that you cannot escape. You feel directed to do something.

2. **Spiritual Ear**- Your spirit man has ears that are designed to **hear** the word of the Lord.

Behold, I stand at the door, and knock: if any man hear my voice, and open the door, I will come in to him, and will sup with him, and he with me. To him that overcometh will I grant to sit with me in my throne, even as I also overcame, and am set down with my Father in his throne. He that hath an ear, let him hear what the Spirit saith unto the churches. (Revelation 3:20-22)

And he said, Go forth, and stand upon the mount before the Lord. And, behold, the Lord passed by, and a great and strong wind rent the mountains, and brake in pieces the rocks before the Lord; but the Lord was not in the wind: and after the wind an earthquake; but the Lord was not in the earthquake: And after the earthquake a fire; but the Lord was not in the fire: and after the fire a still small voice. (1 Kings 19:11-12)

Experiences of Spiritual Hearing:

- Voice of the Lord- when you clearly hear the Lord speak to you whether that is a whisper as in the still small voice, a thundering voice or the audible voice of God.
- Instructions spoken to inner man- this is like an inner conversation. You hear the direction of the Lord released to you as a voice inside of you.

3. **Spiritual Eyes**- Vision is released to the eyes of your spirit. *(Ephesians 1:18)*. Your spiritual eyes were created to see into the invisible realm. All visual prophetic communication is in this category.

While we look not at the things which are seen, but at the things which are not seen: for the things which are seen are temporal; but the things which are not seen are eternal. (2 Corinthians 4:18)

Three Types of Visions:
- Open Vision
- Inner Vision
- Night Vision

We will define and discuss these in greater detail further in this writing.

Many times in my ministry the Lord has used my spirit eyes to reveal something of vital importance to me. I can recall several occasions when I experienced an inner vision where it was as if I was watching a movie clip of a service. I saw myself praying for certain people and knew exactly what the Lord wanted to do. When I would show up to minister, I would simply do what the Lord had already revealed and His power would come to me in a great way!

A prophetic spirit will help you and your family. People misunderstand prophetic ministry and think it is just for a service or church life. The truth is that as your spirit eyes, ears and mind begin receiving heavenly downloads, it brings direction in your life.

Many people fail to realize that there is a place called "there." "There" is right in the middle of the will of God for your life! I can look back at bold steps of obedience in my life when the Lord led me to relocate to do something radical for Him and every time that step of obedience brought great blessing to many areas of my life.

We need a prophetic spirit to have successful marriages. The leading of the Holy Spirit upon a couple can bring joy and breakthrough. We need the word of knowledge and wisdom to raise children. We can parent our children supernaturally!

There is a prophetic anointing upon people for business and investing. God knows exactly what stock is going up and what is going down. He knows everything that the future holds and His marketplace ministers can be led by His Spirit to walk in supernatural abundance and favor.

Every Pastor needs a measure of the prophetic spirit to guide their steps and shine the light of God upon their preaching! Truthfully, no matter what we are called to do for God, a good dose of illumination will empower us to go the distance and avoid unnecessary traps along the way.

CHAPTER 3

Prophets and Miracles

The Prophet's ministry is a miracle ministry. Prophets consistently walk in divine revelation. As they move in the flow of the Spirit, there is a release of supernatural power!

Miracle of Multiplication:

And the word of the Lord came unto him, saying, Arise, get thee to Zarephath, which belongeth to Zidon, and dwell there: behold, I have commanded a widow woman there to sustain thee. So he arose and went to Zarephath. And when he came to the gate of the city, behold, the widow woman was there gathering of sticks: and he called to her, and said, Fetch me, I pray thee, a little water in a vessel, that I may drink. And as she was going to fetch it, he called to her, and said, Bring me, I pray thee, a morsel of bread in thine hand. And she said, As the Lord thy God liveth, I have not a cake, but an handful of meal in a barrel, and a little oil in a cruse: and,

behold, I am gathering two sticks, that I may go in and dress it for me and my son, that we may eat it, and die. And Elijah said unto her, Fear not; go and do as thou hast said: but make me thereof a little cake first, and bring it unto me, and after make for thee and for thy son. For thus saith the Lord God of Israel, The barrel of meal shall not waste, neither shall the cruse of oil fail, until the day that the Lord sendeth rain upon the earth. And she went and did according to the saying of Elijah: and she, and he, and her house, did eat many days. And the barrel of meal wasted not, neither did the cruse of oil fail, according to the word of the Lord, which he spake by Elijah. (1 Kings 17:8-16)

Elijah had been led by God to the brook Cherith during a time of famine where he was fed supernaturally by the ravens. One day when the brook dried up, a **second word** from the Lord came to him to get up and move! One powerful thing about receiving prophetic direction is that it can unlock protection and provision. Elijah was directed by God to go to the brook; that was the **first word** but when the brook dried up he did not just sit there and die! He sought the Lord and there came a **second word**.

Many believers miss it because they do not tune their ears into the **second word.** They wrongly assume that because God said one thing they just stay there even if it is drying up. The prophetic spirit is a progressive spirit that keeps moving and seeking! It does not just stay in some dead place because it is comfortable. In fact, prophetic people will be drawn away from ministries that have dried up and lost the flow because they are created to live in the flow.

Elijah was sent to Zarephath to receive provision. Upon arrival he meets a destitute widow woman who has lost all hope. The word of the Lord comes to him that she is to provide for him. He declares an impossible word and hope arises in her heart to overtake fear. She obeys the prophetic word and there is a miracle of **multiplication** and **provision.**

True prophetic ministry holds great power and can override natural law. God's spoken word releases faith and power. Prophetic ministry will sometimes declare things so contrary to the natural circumstance that the only people who can agree with it are those who are deeply planted in the Spirit.

The miracle was birthed by the Prophet's obedience to go and then speak the word. It was completed when the widow woman **partnered** with the word. What would have happened if she had ignored his word? Her provision would have dried up; she would have died and God would have sent him elsewhere. Had that happened, people could have accused him of delivering a false prophecy. However, the truth is that personal prophetic words require obedience and partnership. Personal prophetic words are often conditional. We have to partner with the word, obey any instruction given and flow in God's will in order for the promise to be made fully manifest.

Miracle of Fire:

Elijah squared off against the false prophets in the land by challenging them to build an altar to their gods. He built an altar to the Living God and they all called down fire. Only Yahweh, Jehovah God Almighty, answered with a powerful fire from heaven, consuming the sacrifice and proving the undeniable reality of God.

Elijah's bold faith and strong prophetic ministry revealed the power of the Living God to the nation of Israel. In a single day there was national reform and the evil prophets who sought false gods were slain.

> *And it came to pass at the time of the offering of the evening sacrifice, that Elijah the prophet came near, and said, Lord God of Abraham, Isaac, and of Israel, let it be known this day that thou art God in Israel, and that I am thy servant, and that I have done all these things at thy word. Hear me, O Lord, hear me, that this people may know that thou art the Lord God, and that thou hast turned their heart back again. Then the fire of the Lord fell, and consumed the burnt sacrifice, and the wood, and the stones, and the dust, and licked up the water that was in the trench. And when all the people saw it, they fell on their faces: and they said, The Lord, he is the God; the Lord, he is the God. (1 Kings 18:36-39)*

The Parting of the Waters of the Jordan:

> *And Elijah took his mantle, and wrapped it together, and smote the waters, and they were divided hither and thither, so that they two went over on dry ground. (2 Kings 2:8)*

As Elijah was preparing to be taken up in the whirlwind, he came to the Jordan River and parted the waters supernaturally. The laws of the Spirit can override natural laws.

True prophets are very in tune with the spirit realm and have no problem believing for and manifesting the miraculous, whether it be a miracle of healing, provision or supernatural help!

The Healing of the Waters:

> *And he went forth unto the spring of the waters, and cast the salt in there, and said, Thus saith the Lord, I have healed these waters; there shall not be from thence any more death or barren land. So the waters were healed unto this day, according to the saying of Elisha which he spake. (2 Kings 2:21-22)*

Immediately after Elijah had been taken up, desperate people from a city that had contamination in the water sought the prophetic ministry of Elisha. Why would they seek a Prophet for such a thing? Because they knew that the Prophet walked in supernatural power and flowed in the realm of the miraculous.

Elisha poured salt into the spring and **spoke** over the water and it was healed! The impurity and contamination was removed supernaturally. One of the dominant functions of the prophetic ministry is speaking and declaring. Prophets declare the word of the Lord and that declaration releases power. There is a powerful anointing in the mouth of a Prophet. Prophetic people have to put a watch over their mouths and be cautious about what they speak. Words are seeds and carry weight in the realm of the spirit.

Multiplication of Oil and Release of Provision:

Now there cried a certain woman of the wives of the sons of the prophets unto Elisha, saying, Thy servant my husband is dead; and thou knowest that thy servant did fear the Lord: and the creditor is come to take unto him my two sons to be bondmen. And Elisha said unto her, What shall I do for thee? tell me, what hast thou in the house? And she said, Thine handmaid hath not any thing in the house, save a pot of oil. Then he said, Go, borrow thee vessels abroad of all thy neighbours, even empty vessels; borrow not a few. And when thou art come in, thou shalt shut the door upon thee and upon thy sons, and shalt pour out into all those vessels, and thou shalt set aside that which is full. So she went from him, and shut the door upon her and upon her sons, who brought the vessels to her; and she poured out. And it came to pass, when the vessels were full, that she said unto her son, Bring me yet a vessel. And he said unto her, There is not a vessel more. And the oil stayed. Then she came and told the man of God. And he said, Go, sell the oil, and pay thy debt, and live thou and thy children of the rest. (2 Kings 4:1-7)

Elisha finds a desperate woman whose husband has died and she is about to lose her sons. The devil loves to attack people on multiple fronts. He never sends an attack that only affects one area. He always releases demonic schemes that have the potential to affect a person on several levels. He was trying to defeat this woman and destroy her family.

Elisha releases a very simple prophetic instruction to her! His words actually make very little sense. He tells her to go and gather vessels and then pour into them the only thing that is in her house of any value, her oil. What if she ignored him or thought that these were foolish words?

She obeyed the instruction of the Prophet which released supernatural multiplication, provision and debt cancellation in her house! The prophetic word aborted the plans of the enemy. Prophets can be great instruments of power, tearing down the works of darkness.

Resurrection of the Shunammite Woman's Son:

And when Elisha was come into the house, behold, the child was dead, and laid upon his bed. He went in therefore, and shut the door upon them twain, and prayed unto the Lord. And he went up, and lay upon the child, and put his mouth upon his mouth, and his eyes upon his eyes, and his hands upon his hands: and he stretched himself upon the child; and the flesh of the child waxed warm. Then he returned, and walked in the house to and fro; and went up, and stretched himself upon him: and the child sneezed seven times, and the child opened his eyes. And he called Gehazi, and said, Call this Shunammite. So he called her. And when she was come in unto him, he said, Take up thy son. Then she went in, and fell at his feet, and bowed herself to the ground, and took up her son, and went out. (2 Kings 4:32-37)

This woman was a partner with the ministry of Elisha. She perceived the power upon his ministry which led her to help him by providing a place to stay and taking care of him when he was in her area. The woman and her husband had become a great help to Elisha's traveling ministry.

On a particular day Elisha feels compelled to do something for this woman. I do not believe this was just a thought in his head but a leading of the Spirit. God wanted to reward this woman's seed. There is a great lesson here: we can draw from wells that we have helped dig! Another way of saying it is, we can harvest where we have sown. When God puts us in divine partnership with certain gifts, we can expect a harvest of the strength, power and ability of that office. This woman had been sowing into the life of a Prophet and she was about to receive a Prophet's reward.

Elisha discovered that the lady had been barren. She seemed to have all that a person could want: a good marriage, a prosperous financial condition, a place of influence and esteem in society. Still there was a vacant place in her heart. There was a deep desire which had been suppressed long ago because she could not bear any more disappointment in that area. She deeply wanted to be a mother yet her body had not managed to conceive and bear a child.

One dimension of the prophetic anointing is resurrection power. Prophetic words will sometimes speak to the deepest parts of us and awaken things that seemed to have long ago gone away. Prophetic words can bring life to the dead areas of our own heart, mind and faith.

Elisha delivered a very clear word to the woman; she was going to get pregnant and bear a child! She was shocked and a bit scared. She pleaded with the Prophet not to get her hopes up and he assured her that it was a done deal! According to his word her womb was opened. She conceived and bore a beautiful son that filled the deep longing in her heart.

One day her son fell ill and died upon her lap! Can you imagine the pain of feeling as though your life was finally complete and your heart's desire granted only to have it all ripped away? Many people would have grown angry and bitter with God but this woman had a deep inner strength and faith that arose. She immediately remembered the promise of the man of God. She laid her son on his bed, rode to where the man of God was and demanded that he come to her house. She refused to speak a negative word and would not give up until he agreed to come.

I believe that this story is one of the great faith stories of the Bible. The woman partnered so deep with the promise that even in a time of severe crisis she was holding God to His word. She absolutely refused to accept the report of the enemy. God was faithful and her son was healed!

The Floating Axehead:

And the sons of the prophets said unto Elisha, Behold now, the place where we dwell with thee is too strait for us. Let us go, we pray thee, unto Jordan, and take thence every man a beam, and let us make us a place there, where we may dwell. And he answered, Go ye. And one said, Be content, I pray thee, and go with thy servants. And he answered, I will go. So he went with them. And when

they came to Jordan, they cut down wood. But as one was felling a beam, the axe head fell into the water: and he cried, and said, Alas, master! for it was borrowed. And the man of God said, Where fell it? And he shewed him the place. And he cut down a stick, and cast it in thither; and the iron did swim. Therefore said he, Take it up to thee. And he put out his hand, and took it. (2 Kings 6:1-6)

The power of God caused iron to swim! In a moment there was a transformation that recovered a missing axehead. God's power transformed the molecular structure of the iron and water causing the axehead to float to the surface. This miracle met the need and recovered the axehead.

The Healing of Naaman:

So Naaman came with his horses and with his chariot, and stood at the door of the house of Elisha. And Elisha sent a messenger unto him, saying, Go and wash in Jordan seven times, and thy flesh shall come again to thee, and thou shalt be clean. But Naaman was wroth, and went away, and said, Behold, I thought, He will surely come out to me, and stand, and call on the name of the Lord his God, and strike his hand over the place, and recover the leper. Are not Abana and Pharpar, rivers of Damascus, better than all the waters of Israel? may I not wash in them, and be clean? So he turned and went away in a rage. And his servants came near, and spake unto him, and said, My father, if the prophet had bid thee do some great thing, wouldest thou not have done it? how

much rather then, when he saith to thee, Wash, and be clean? Then went he down, and dipped himself seven times in Jordan, according to the saying of the man of God: and his flesh came again like unto the flesh of a little child, and he was clean. And he returned to the man of God, he and all his company, and came, and stood before him: and he said, Behold, now I know that there is no God in all the earth, but in Israel: now therefore, I pray thee, take a blessing of thy servant. (2 Kings 5:9-15)

The healing ministry is one of the most powerful dimensions of prophetic ministry. When the word of knowledge flows and God reveals a condition in a person's body, His goal is to bring supernatural healing. The healing ministry is a gift to the Church, ministering to God's people and releasing His promises to them.

Healing ministry is an evangelism tool for the lost. It is amazing how a heart opens up when God gives a believer a word of knowledge for a lost person, reveals a condition in their mind or body and then heals the condition! It doesn't take a long sermon after that type of encounter to get the person saved.

Naaman needed a miracle. Prophets are unusual people and tend to be much more God-minded than people-minded. They can easily come across in an offensive manner because of their personality.

Naaman was initially offended by how Elisha handled his request and the word that he had given him. This reveals another fascinating dimension of prophetic ministry. Many times the prophetic word and instruction that a person receives will actually challenge them. It comes down to a simple question: how hungry are we?

I will never forget an experience that I had which shook me. I went to Bible college as a bound up seventeen year old who had an encounter with God and wanted to pursue His plans for my life. I knew that there were many areas of my life in which I desperately needed freedom. Shortly after I arrived at school, I received a prophetic word during morning prayer. The minister spoke about my need for freedom and released the power of God over me. I could feel chains breaking and freedom flowing.

When I got home that day, the enemy began to sow seeds of doubt into my heart in an attempt to steal the word. He began to stir embarrassment in me and tell me that the other students would judge me and not accept me because I was receiving freedom prayer in front of everyone. Suddenly, the Lord spoke deep into my heart and asked me how bad I wanted to be free! I realized right then that the encounter I had was an invitation to freedom and I was not going to let the devil steal it. That was a turning point in my life. I realized that the fear of the Lord must always outweigh the fear of man. When we really want to be free, we don't care what it takes.

Naaman faced the same challenge. His miracle came to him in a package that he didn't like. Isn't it ridiculous that we would miss our breakthrough over something as silly as how it was delivered? Desperate people do not care! They want Jesus and His freedom any way they can get it.

Thank God that Naaman had someone in his life who did not fuel his offense but encouraged him to get free! Many times fleshly people are used by the devil in our lives to fuel critical spirits and carnal thinking in order to steal the word from our lives and keep us bound. If Naaman had the type of friends that many Christians today have they would have joined in his offense, judged the man of God and aborted the plan for a miracle!

Miracles come in all kinds of packages. Who cares what the wrapping paper looks like if there is a breakthrough on the inside? Naaman's prophetic word made no sense in the natural! Sometimes you have to obey a seemingly silly instruction in order to get the breakthrough. Naaman was encouraged to obey God. As he did, the Prophet's word produced healing in his flesh and rescued him from a lifetime of sickness and defeat.

Prophets are people called to the miraculous. They carry a strong spirit of insight that gives birth to miracles. Prophetic people believe in the impossible and see into the invisible!

CHAPTER 4

Understanding and Defining the Gift of Prophecy

Now there are diversities of gifts, but the same Spirit. And there are differences of administrations, but the same Lord. And there are diversities of operations, but it is the same God which worketh all in all. But the manifestation of the Spirit is given to every man to profit withal. For to one is given by the Spirit the word of wisdom; to another the word of knowledge by the same Spirit; To another faith by the same Spirit; to another the gifts of healing by the same Spirit; To another the working of miracles; to another prophecy; to another discerning of spirits; to another divers kinds of tongues; to another the interpretation of tongues: But all these worketh that one and the self-same Spirit, dividing to every man severally as he will. (1 Corinthians 12:4-11)

The nine gifts of the Spirit are supernatural power tools that bring explosive results in the life of a believer. One of the key dimensions of the person of the Holy Spirit is that He is our helper (*John 14:26*). The divine ministry of the Holy Spirit brings supernatural help!

These gifts were not merely given to preachers or ministers but to the entire Body of Christ. Every member has access to the gifts and ministries of the Holy Spirit. In Charismatic circles confusion often comes because people mistake the resident ministry of the Holy Spirit in the life of a believer for the call into a five-fold office. The truth is that **all believers** can function in the gifts of the Spirit, including the gift of prophecy. The functioning of the gift of prophecy in the life of a believer is much different than the functioning of the gift of prophecy in the ministry of a Prophet.

We can look at the gift of teaching for example. There are many wonderful believers who love God's word and can sit with a struggling person and share truths with them that help them understand the Father's plan. That does not mean that they are going to be flying all over the world functioning in the five-fold ministry gift of the Teacher.

Believers have access to the fullness of God and can function in many different spiritual gifts but that does not mean that they have the grace upon their lives to function in a five-fold capacity. This is especially true concerning the gift of prophecy. Many people automatically assume that because they have given a few prophetic words that ministered to people, then surely they are called to be a Prophet. This is a dangerous assumption that is responsible for much of the trouble and conflict in the local church concerning prophecy.

The simple gift of prophecy is available to the entire Body. What is the simple gift of prophecy that every believer can function in?

But he that prophesieth speaketh unto men to edification, and exhortation, and comfort.
(1 Corinthians 14:3)

Three Components of the Simple Gift of Prophecy:

1. **Edify**...to build up.
   When a prophetic word is released over a people or an individual it releases hope and builds up.
2. **Exhort**...encourage and strengthen.
   The gift of prophecy can bring great strength to the life of a person. The very words are infused with life and power!
3. **Comfort**... ministering to the heart.
   The gift of prophecy can speak peace over a storm, healing over a wound and vision over the discouraged. When the gift of prophecy is accurately flowing, there is such comfort to know that God is speaking right where you are and showing vision for the future!

The simple gift of prophecy should really be active in the life of a believer. One of the cornerstones of the Christian life should be daily prayer. Prayer is never intended to be a monologue but a dialogue.

- *Seek the Lord and his strength, seek his face continually. (1 Chronicles 16:11)*
- *I love them that love me; and those that seek me early shall find me. (Proverbs 8:17)*

- **My sheep hear my voice, and I know them, and they follow me. (John 10:27)**
- **I will hear what God the Lord will speak: for he will speak peace unto his people, and to his saints: but let them not turn again to folly. (Psalm 85:8)**

Prayer should consist of seeking, worshipping, praying in the Spirit, interceding and then **listening.** That is really one of the vital keys of living a prophetic life: **tuning out the natural and tuning into the Spirit.** The religious spirit has convinced so many believers that they cannot hear from God yet as sons we should be receiving instruction on a regular basis.

I remember when the Lord first began to visit me with the simple gift of prophecy. I had experienced a life-changing encounter with God at sixteen years old. I immediately started to attend prayer meetings. Sometimes at these meetings I would feel something like a dam breaking open deep in my belly. I really had no idea what was going on. Eventually I began to give prophetic words in the prayer group under the direction of the leadership. I learned that what I was feeling was the flow inside of me.

I hungered so deeply to hear from God and walk with Him. I began to take long walks outside all alone with God and cry out to Him. His power and presence increased upon my life. He began to form in me a prophetic ministry that would continue to grow and prosper through the years. During that time of formation, I would slip into other realms of tongues in my prayer closet and began to ask God for interpretation. The Lord started giving me tongues and interpretations in my private times with Him. He was training me for a supernatural ministry that would unfold in unbelievable ways.

My prayer closet became my training ground! If you want to sharpen your prophetic senses, do it in your prayer time. Learn to tune into the Spirit realm and hear the voice of the Father. It is scary to see how many people long to give a prophetic word on a microphone in front of a group but have very little accurate prophetic function in their own prayer life.

One of the things that I have learned to do through the years is to journal my prayer times. As you spend alone time with God, listen for His voice and write down what He says. Carry something with you into your prayer time and be ready to write anything that comes to you. This is a vital tool in sharpening your prophetic leading.

The simple gift of prophecy can function in a church gathering through believers. The leadership of a ministry can follow the guidelines given in First Corinthians chapter fourteen to allow prophetic words to flow as they feel led. The words coming from believers will typically follow the three guidelines of simple prophecy: edifying, exhorting and comforting. This is much different than a prophetic presbytery established by apostolic leadership to provide prophetic insight into the church.

A prophetic presbytery is made of people who have demonstrated a genuine prophetic calling, not just prophetic believers functioning in the simple gift of prophecy. They have been established by the governing leadership of the house to provide a deeper dimension of prophetic ministry.

Prophets function on a much more intense level of prophetic ministry. Most Prophets have had experiences where they began to see things and hear things that they may not have understood until they received revelation and instruction concerning their prophetic calling.

One of the cornerstones of the Prophet's ministry is **revelation.** The nine gifts of the Spirit are broken down into three major categories:

1. Revelation Gifts-
   Word of Knowledge
   Word of Wisdom
   Discerning of Spirits
2. Power Gifts-
   The Gift of Faith
   The Working of Miracles
   The Gift of Healing(s)
3. The Vocal Gifts-
   The Gift of Prophecy
   Tongues and Interpretation
   Diverse Tongues

A Prophet will have a very active flow of one or more of the revelation gifts. A believer may occasionally get a word of knowledge or a word of wisdom but a Prophet lives in that realm. When a Prophet speaks prophetically to the people of God it is not the simple gift of prophecy but they speak from a deeper level of revelation, insight and authority. They bring words to the Body and the nations that are revelatory words.

All five-fold ministry gifts must have a preaching and teaching ministry. Some will flow very strong in the supernatural gifts of God but they must be able to communicate His word to the people. Prophets may spend a lot of time releasing individual or corporate prophetic words but they must also be able to declare the written word. Most Prophets will preach and teach in a very prophetic manner. They bring things out from the word that seem to speak right into the situation of the hearer in a much different way than a Teacher or Pastor would. A Prophet's message usually challenges the heart of the hearer and reveals dimensions of the Father that the person has been struggling to receive.

A Prophet has a lifestyle of intimacy and seeking. He or she is most at home in the presence of God. By nature a Prophet is an intercessor, spending a lot of time seeking God for others. Prophets are people of presence. When a Prophet speaks, they often call people to greater intimacy with God.

Another realm of the Prophetic Gift is **predictive prophecy.** This is a word that speaks about something that is coming but has not yet manifested. Throughout history God has used the prophetic ministry to declare things that are coming. Prophets often foretell future events. Many times when these types of words are given, it can be very easy to brush them aside because there may be no natural indicator.

God used Elijah and at his word rain ceased and a great drought gripped the land for three and a half years:

And Elijah the Tishbite, who was of the inhabitants of Gilead, said unto Ahab, As the Lord God of Israel

liveth, before whom I stand, there shall not be dew nor rain these years, but according to my word. (1 Kings 17:1)

At the end of that time, God used Elijah to call forth the rain and bring an end to the drought! When he spoke the word he appeared very foolish because there was no sign of rain in the land but the Prophet had faith and declared the word of the Lord. The atmosphere shifted and the drought came to a sudden end!

And it came to pass after many days, that the word of the Lord came to Elijah in the third year, saying, Go, shew thyself unto Ahab; and I will send rain upon the earth. (1 Kings 18:1)

And Elijah said unto Ahab, Get thee up, eat and drink; for there is a sound of abundance of rain. So Ahab went up to eat and to drink. And Elijah went up to the top of Carmel; and he cast himself down upon the earth, and put his face between his knees, And said to his servant, Go up now, look toward the sea. And he went up, and looked, and said, There is nothing. And he said, Go again seven times. And it came to pass at the seventh time, that he said, Behold, there ariseth a little cloud out of the sea, like a man's hand. And he said, Go up, say unto Ahab, Prepare thy chariot, and get thee down, that the rain stop thee not. And it came to pass in the mean while, that the heaven was black with clouds and wind, and there was a great rain. And Ahab rode, and went to Jezreel. And the hand of the Lord was on Elijah; and he girded up his loins, and ran before Ahab to the entrance of Jezreel. (1 Kings 18:41-46)

Other examples of predictive prophesy in the Bible:
- Elijah prophesied that Ahab's sons would all be destroyed *(1 Kings 21:22)*
- Elijah predicted that Jezebel would be eaten by dogs *(1 Kings 21:23)*
- Elijah declared that Ahaziah would die of his illness *(2 Kings 1:4)*
- Elisha prophesied the end of the great famine *(2 Kings 7:1)*
- Elisha predicted a seven-year famine *(2 Kings 8:1)*
- Elisha prophesied Benhadad's untimely death *(2 Kings 8:10)*
- Agabus prophesied a great famine. *(Acts 11:27-30)*

God uses the office of the Prophet to give warnings to individuals, groups, ministries, regions and even nations. One of the most profound examples of a prophetic warning in the New Testament is the Prophet Agabus warning Paul of impending danger:

And as we tarried there many days, there came down from Judaea a certain prophet, named Agabus. And when he was come unto us, he took Paul's girdle, and bound his own hands and feet, and said, Thus saith the Holy Ghost, So shall the Jews at Jerusalem bind the man that owneth this girdle, and shall deliver him into the hands of the Gentiles. (Acts 21:10-11)

Prophets live in a realm of seeking and seeing. The Lord often reveals unseen dangers to them. Many times I have seen the prophetic ministry pinpoint something hidden in the heart of a person that is intended to be a tool of the enemy. Immature believers may find prophetic warnings offensive or negative but it is actually an expression of the love of God.

My son, despise not the chastening of the Lord; neither be weary of his correction: For whom the Lord loveth he correcteth; even as a father the son in whom he delighteth. (Proverbs 3:11-12)

For whom the Lord loveth he chasteneth, and scourgeth every son whom he receiveth. If ye endure chastening, God dealeth with you as with sons; for what son is he whom the father chasteneth not? But if ye be without chastisement, whereof all are partakers, then are ye bastards, and not sons. Furthermore we have had fathers of our flesh which corrected us, and we gave them reverence: shall we not much rather be in subjection unto the Father of spirits, and live? For they verily for a few days chastened us after their own pleasure; but he for our profit, that we might be partakers of his holiness. Now no chastening for the present seemeth to be joyous, but grievous: nevertheless afterward it yieldeth the peaceable fruit of righteousness unto them which are exercised thereby. (Hebrews 12:6-11)

God is a good Father! Part of the fathering nature of God is providing correction and lovingly pruning away things that are holding us back. One of the controversial dimensions of the prophetic anointing is rebuke and correction. The truth is that the Prophet's office is one that is called to release the heart of God to the Bride. Many times Prophets may speak of plans and encourage but there are also times when a r word will be much more of a rebuke, warning or cor

The seasoned Prophet does not take pleasure in rebuke. I once heard it said that the dilemma of the Prophet is not just what you see but what to do with what you see. Many young Prophets simply run to and fro blasting and never building. They actually enjoy issuing rebuke and correction. This simply reveals their immaturity. A seasoned Prophet weeps over the condition of people and wants to see them rise into all that the Father has.

Many times it is not the word that is delivered that causes wounds in the hearts of people but **how** the word was delivered. Prophets and prophetic people must learn how to steward the insight that God gives and deliver it in the proper way.

The Body of Christ must also be matured to understand that warnings or corrections are not negative but actually God's arm of divine protection moving in the life of a believer. Prophetic warnings can cut off the plans of the enemy and rescue a person from much difficulty **if those warnings are heeded!**

The Prophets are God's trumpets! The trumpet is created to **release the sound,** calling God's people to attention. Oftentimes the trumpet releases a sound of warning to alert God's people. Prophets are called to **expose** and **reveal.**

Cry aloud, spare not, lift up thy voice like a trumpet, and shew my people their transgression, and the house of Jacob their sins. (Isaiah 58:1)

Blow ye the trumpet in Zion, and sound an alarm in my holy mountain: let all the inhabitants of the land

tremble: for the day of the Lord cometh, for it is nigh at hand. (Joel 2:1)

One role of the Prophet is God's watchman. The Lord takes the prophetic office and sets it in the high places in the Spirit, revealing mysteries. Prophets have divine ability to see things that others may not see. This is one reason why Prophets are so important in the lives of Apostles.

The Apostle is very focused on the **plans** for transformation and **Kingdom advance.** Apostles are governing gifts in the Body who are granted much wisdom and favor but are also gifts that are very focused on the work at hand. The Apostle can miss an attack or plot because they are focused on the **mission.** This is why the Prophet is vital in the life and work of an Apostle.

Again the word of the Lord came unto me, saying, Son of man, speak to the children of thy people, and say unto them, When I bring the sword upon a land, if the people of the land take a man of their coasts, and set him for their watchman: If when he seeth the sword come upon the land, he blow the trumpet, and warn the people; Then whosoever heareth the sound of the trumpet, and taketh not warning; if the sword come, and take him away, his blood shall be upon his own head. He heard the sound of the trumpet, and took not warning; his blood shall be upon him. But he that taketh warning shall deliver his soul. But if the watchman see the sword come, and blow not the trumpet, and the people be not warned; if the sword come,

and take any person from among them, he is taken away in his iniquity; but his blood will I require at the watchman's hand. So thou, O son of man, I have set thee a watchman unto the house of Israel; therefore thou shalt hear the word at my mouth, and warn them from me. (Ezekiel 33:1-7)

There are many self-appointed Prophets who enter into local churches or ministries in an attempt to establish themselves as watchmen. This can easily give way to a controlling and dominating spirit that creates problems. I have seen persons who claim to be prophetic enter a ministry and bring extreme division and challenge because they refuse to submit to the God-appointed leadership. They claim to be watchmen who know better than the leaders or Pastor. This is an error in thinking and believing. God does not send His people to create rebellion. Much of the time this happens because a person misunderstands the role of a watchman.

The first thing to note is that the concept of a watchman was given to the Prophet Ezekiel. This was not written to a believer who flows in the simple gift of prophecy. This was not written to an intercessory prayer team. This was written to a Prophet. That is an important distinction because the office bears a different measure of authority and grace.

God uses the Prophet to be like a mighty trumpet, warning the people of God concerning the enemy's plans. Prophets may give strong warnings to churches. I have ministered alongside Prophets many times as they observed something about a person that I missed. Their warning saved me much trouble! Thank God for prophetic warnings.

Typically the Pastor, Apostle or local church leader has invited the Prophet to speak into their life and the life of the church. In that situation the Prophet has been granted authority to release words of warning or correction as needed. There are different ways in which such words should be delivered. For example, a very specific word about leaders in a local church may be much better received and delivered in a private setting than in public. Releasing a word in an improper manner has the potential to abort the assignment upon that word and create unnecessary conflict.

Intercessory prayer groups can become a powerful force in the life of a church. As the prayer team's heart becomes knit with the vision of the house and the leaders, they will begin to receive insight and revelation regarding the ministry, adding fuel to their prayers. It is really impossible to spend much time praying for a person or ministry without beginning to receive insight for them. The team must use caution and remember that they are submitted to the leaders of the house, walking alongside of them, not placing themselves above.

I have seen prayer teams take on a sense of elitism and begin to operate in rebellion. It is certainly true that they may pick up on some things in the Spirit that needs to be shared with their senior leader as a word of warning or caution. They must, however, demonstrate humility and grace in sharing the word and allow that leader to take it before the Lord and seek God for how to steward it. If the prayer team begins to get direction that differs with that of the leaders of the house, there can be room given for false spirits to enter in and create havoc.

Members of a church should not come in and take on the mentality that they are watchmen over the church to receive vision and direction on a greater level than the Pastor or leader.

This maneuver is out of order and inspired by the enemy. Again, the concept of a watchman is referring to the **office of a Prophet** not necessarily a prophetic believer.

I know that prophetic believers can receive some really powerful revelations for their leaders and their ministry. When this stream is flowing properly it will actually bring refreshing to the leadership. If it is not flowing properly, it can cause severe problems.

God has appointed His Apostles and Pastors to **govern** local churches along with those that they have appointed. He has entrusted the care of the sheep to those that He has appointed to lead them. Mature believers who receive prophetic insight gladly bring it to the appointed leadership and **submit** it to them. They do not try to ram it down their throat or **govern** through their prophetic words. A prophetic church can be a place of such powerful ministry, releasing healing, direction and prayer but it takes teaching, training and much grace to get there!

Another realm of prophetic utterance is the gift of tongues and interpretation as found in First Corinthians chapter twelve. In this flow, God gives a person a message in an unknown tongue. It comes bubbling up in their inner man. It is a message that holds great value for the intended audience. When this happens in a public service it is to edify, exhort and comfort those who will receive the message. It can reveal things to hearers that are of vital importance to them for that moment. Tongues and interpretation builds up the Body! When tongues and interpretation flow together it is the equivalent of prophecy.

There is a right way to deliver a message in an unknown tongue. Many times in Charismatic and Pentecostal services an inexperienced person will feel the bubbling sensation deep in their belly and just blurt out a loud message in tongues with no interpreter present. That is the wrong way to do it! There are also times in a corporate gathering when a person becomes overwhelmed by the ministry of the Holy Spirit and has a deep encounter with God that brings an eruption of loud praying in tongues and rejoicing. These tongues are not for the audience but for them. That is an entirely different matter.

In the upper room there were tongues like fire resting upon the people *(Acts 2:3-4)*. Think about that for a moment, tongues as fire! Do you think they were being quiet? No way. The mighty burning of the Holy Spirit was upon them igniting things deep within. There is a reason why the religious people thought they were drunk! I believe it was because there were many wild signs of Spirit-filled encounters. When a believer has a powerful encounter with the Holy Spirit they may be loud and unusual but this is not to be quickly judged and rejected.

If any man speak in an unknown tongue, let it be by two, or at the most by three, and that by course; and let one interpret. But if there be no interpreter, let him keep silence in the church; and let him speak to himself, and to God. (1 Corinthians 14:27-28)

Paul is addressing messages in tongues in a public gathering. A person who receives an unction to give a message in an unknown tongue should not do so if there is no one to interpret. It will not bless and strengthen the people in the meeting without proper interpretation. Many times if God begins to use a person in public messages in tongues they will develop the capacity to interpret. It is actually something that a person can seek for if God is using them in that way. The deliverer of a message has the responsibility of properly stewarding it.

In a public setting the first thing to do is to seek the permission of whoever is in charge of the service. Many times they may know if someone is there who has the ability to interpret. They may also have a sense of the right timing to deliver the message. Again, if there is no one to interpret then Paul advises to hold it. There is such a heavenly blessing when these two gifts flow in a meeting and release tender words from heaven!

The interpretation of other tongues is not direct word-for-word translation. It is the showing forth of the message given. For example, someone might speak in tongues for fifteen minutes and the interpretation may only be five minutes long. It has absolutely nothing to do with length of time but with accurately interpreting the mind of the Lord. I have also seen prophetic ministers speak in tongues and then bring teaching or have a prayer line. I believe those things can serve as an interpretation of what was declared in the Spirit as well.

CHAPTER 5

Dreams and Visions

Dreams and visions are a part of the prophetic ministry. In fact, Prophets often have the gift of interpreting dreams. God often speaks to His people through dreams but it is vital to record the dream, write it down and get proper interpretation of the meaning. God never visits someone with a prophetic dream without having a specific purpose.

I can recall several times that God has given me dreams to provide guidance for me or others. One time I went to sleep and had a dream about two friends who were Associate Pastors. In my dream their Pastor was resigning but the Lord said it was going to be alright. The next day they called my wife and me and left us a voicemail. They did not say what they wanted but asked us to call them. I had not told my wife about the dream so before we called I told her that I knew what they wanted and told her the details. When we called them, that was exactly what happened and we were able to minster to them because the word of the Lord had already come to us.

Many times in my life I have had warning dreams and visions. The Lord has shown me hidden plans of evil or deception in a situation and led me to stay away from something that looked like a good opportunity,

One time I had a powerful vision about the healing power of God. The Lord showed me his power displayed like flashes of lightening containing every color imaginable and I saw hands raised up to the Lord and dipping into His power. He told me that many people were not healed because they were waiting upon Him to do something but that He had already paid it all at Calvary and His power was freely available to all who would receive. He told me that people were waiting for a touch from Him while He was waiting for them to reach up and touch Him. I cannot explain in words how this encounter shifted my life and ministry. The reality of God's power gripped me! I preached a couple of days after this vision, shared what God had shown me and He knocked every person in that meeting to the floor. Healing flowed like a river. It was an awe-inspiring display of God's power and glory that was born from a vision in the Spirit realm.

There is a profound ministry in dreams and visions. Many people miss vital instructions because they are not sensitive to the encounters they are having on a regular basis. One of the jobs of the Prophet is to teach and train people about dreams and visions.

Daniel was a Prophet who had the gift of dream interpretation. God used him to reveal His wisdom to people through dreams.

As for these four children, God gave them knowledge and skill in all learning and wisdom: and Daniel had understanding in all visions and dreams. (Daniel 1:17)

Then was the secret revealed unto Daniel in a night vision. Then Daniel blessed the God of heaven. Daniel answered and said, Blessed be the name of God for ever and ever: for wisdom and might are his: And he changeth the times and the seasons: he removeth kings, and setteth up kings: he giveth wisdom unto the wise, and knowledge to them that know understanding: He revealeth the deep and secret things: he knoweth what is in the darkness, and the light dwelleth with him. I thank thee, and praise thee, O thou God of my fathers, who hast given me wisdom and might, and hast made known unto me now what we desired of thee: for thou hast now made known unto us the king's matter. (Daniel 2:19-23)

Prophetic dreams contain vital instruction in the language of our subconscious mind. Many times a prophetic dream will include people and symbols that must be interpreted properly in order to get the right message. We have to sort through the symbolism and not assume that they will be fulfilled literally. One example is the prophetic dream of Joseph in which he saw the sun, moon and eleven stars bowing before him. This was not literally fulfilled but came to pass in the future as his father and eleven brothers bowed before him. *(Genesis 37:5-12; 40:5-22; 44:11-32)*. Dreams are often to be interpreted like parables.

One time I was traveling and had flown to Hawaii. Right before leaving we were negotiating for a building that our ministry needed. It looked as though the deal was done and we would finalize when I returned. I went to sleep one night and had a dream about a plane crash. I woke up very startled and kept thinking about the flight home.

I talked to a good friend and shared my dream. He asked me where I was when the plane crashed in my dream. All of a sudden I realized something so profound. I was watching from the ground and was not in the plane! As we kept talking, he asked me several more questions. By the end of our discussion, we had the meaning. The dream was showing me that something I was working on was going to crash and it looked very distressing but it would be alright. While on that trip the owners of the building backed out of the deal with no good explanation and I knew that the dream I had was preparing my heart for that disappointment. I did not have anxiety about it at all and just knew that God had something even better! Within days, a better building came to us.

Another dream I had one time was a warning for someone else. I dreamt about a man that I knew and that he was having a heart attack. When I woke up I knew that it was not symbolic but a literal warning. I prayed about it and felt a release from the Lord to talk with him. I did not tell him the full dream because I did not want to plant seeds of fear. I had no idea that he had any type of heart issues but when I went to him, he said that he had been under the care of a doctor for heart problems and they had stressed to him to change his diet and lifestyle. I urged him that the word of the Lord was to heed those instructions and take care of his body. He received the word and has gone for years with no trouble.

The ministry of **Visions** is a powerful realm of the prophet-ic ministry. God gives people visions to release wisdom, show what is ahead and give instruction. Prophets operate fairly con-sistently in visions. Revelation is one of the cornerstones of the prophetic ministry. Believers who carry a measure of prophetic operation can also have visions. There are three types of visions:

1. **Open Vision**- this is the highest level of vision. This is when your natural eyes are open and completely over-taken by the spirit realm. A vision unfolds in front of you. You lose track of the natural and see into the spirit realm.

And Balaam lifted up his eyes, and he saw Israel abiding in his tents according to their tribes; and the spirit of God came upon him. And he took up his parable, and said, Balaam the son of Beor hath said, and the man whose eyes are open hath said: He hath said, which heard the words of God, which saw the vision of the Almighty, falling into a trance, but hav-ing his eyes open. (Numbers 24:2-4)

2. **Inner Vision**- this is a vision or picture released into your inner man. You are seeing something inside of your spirit man not with your natural eyes. It often occurs like images blazing across the canvas of your mind's eye.

And Saul arose from the earth; and when his eyes were opened, he saw no man: but they led him by the hand, and brought him into Damascus. And he was three days without sight, and neither did eat nor drink. And there was a certain disciple at Damascus, named Ananias; and to him said the Lord in a vision, Ananias. And he said, Behold, I am here, Lord. And

the Lord said unto him, Arise, and go into the street which is called Straight, and enquire in the house of Judas for one called Saul, of Tarsus: for, behold, he prayeth, And hath seen in a vision a man named Ananias coming in, and putting his hand on him, that he might receive his sight. (Acts 9:8-12)

3. **Night vision-** There is some debate about what a night vision is. Some say it is simply another term for a prophetic dream. Others say that they are two different things altogether, that dreams are more symbolic and visions literal. A vision releases *heavenly insight*. One way of looking at night vision is that it is a release of heavenly insight that comes to a person in the moments between being asleep and awake. A person is somewhere in between the two states when a literal vision comes to them. Many times as your mind becomes quiet and your body relaxes, suddenly your spirit receives a download.

After this I saw in the night visions, and behold a fourth beast, dreadful and terrible, and strong exceedingly; and it had great iron teeth: it devoured and brake in pieces, and stamped the residue with the feet of it: and it was diverse from all the beasts that were before it; and it had ten horns. (Daniel 7:7)

I saw in the night visions, and, behold, one like the Son of man came with the clouds of heaven, and came to the Ancient of days, and they brought him near before him. (Daniel 7:13)

Another type of prophetic encounter is a trance. This is a very misunderstood experience that many people have grown afraid of because of the counterfeit trances that occur in occult practices. Yet, the Bible gives many examples of people receiving visions in a trance state.

A trance is an encounter where the body is in a suspended state similar to a deep sleep. It comes suddenly and unexpectedly. In this state you are not aware of the physical realm but caught up in the spirit realm. A person suddenly falls into a trance (a deep sleep-like state) followed by a return to being wide awake and in full function.

On the morrow, as they went on their journey, and drew nigh unto the city, Peter went up upon the housetop to pray about the sixth hour: And he became very hungry, and would have eaten: but while they made ready, he fell into a trance, And saw heaven opened, and a certain vessel descending unto him, as it had been a great sheet knit at the four corners, and let down to the earth: Wherein were all manner of four footed beasts of the earth, and wild beasts, and creeping things, and fowls of the air. And there came a voice to him, Rise, Peter; kill, and eat. But Peter said, Not so, Lord; for I have never eaten any thing that is common or unclean. And the voice spake unto him again the second time, What God hath cleansed, that call not thou common. This was done thrice: and the vessel was received up again into heaven. Now while Peter doubted in himself what this vision which he had seen should mean, behold, the men which were sent from Cornelius had made enquiry for Simon's house, and stood before the gate, And called, and asked whether Simon, which was surnamed Peter, were lodged there. While

**Peter thought on the vision, the Spirit said unto him,
Behold, three men seek thee. Arise therefore, and
get thee down, and go with them, doubting nothing: for I have sent them. (Acts 10:9-20)**

Peter received a vision during a trance. God was releasing
instruction for him to minister to Cornelius. Prophetic visions
can come to a person during a trance.

**And it came to pass, that, when I was come again
to Jerusalem, even while I prayed in the temple, I
was in a trance; And saw him saying unto me, Make
haste, and get thee quickly out of Jerusalem: for
they will not receive thy testimony concerning me.
(Acts 22:17-18)**

Paul fell into a trance and received a word of warning. God's
divine protection came to Paul while in the trance.

All of these various titles refer to how the vision comes to
a person. The common thread is a **prophetic vision**. The primary difference is the person's physical state while receiving
the vision.

CHAPTER 6

Prophets, the Gift of Prophecy and Prophetic People

The devil hates the power and potential that the prophetic ministry contains. There are many spirits, such as the Jezebel spirit, that actively war against the prophetic. These spirits will hammer a church or ministry that embraces and moves in the prophetic.

Many pastors have grown afraid of the prophetic ministry because of error in the lives of prophetic people. It is always a dangerous stand to take to just cut off an entire ministry gift because of a bad experience. Many of these bad experiences are born from people who have passion and zeal but lack wisdom and training. In their defense, while the Charismatic Church has been good at seeking words and desiring insight, we have often fallen very short in the area of detailed prophetic training and mentorship.

At their core Prophets are God-minded, prayer people who cry out for the word of the Lord and perceive the delivery of that word as the highest calling. Due to the extreme seeking and prayer ministry of most Prophets, they value time away from people and crave extended seasons in the presence of God. By nature they are often bold and confrontational. Many ministry leaders try to strip the boldness and authority away from the Prophets in order to make them more palatable but if they are not cautious about this they could potentially quench some of their fire.

The Church must give permission to Prophets to embrace their true identity. This certainly does not mean lacking love or disregarding order. In fact, most seasoned Prophets develop a great love for the Bride and want to come alongside Pastors and leaders to minister effectively.

The Pastor is a sheep-minded minister who values connection to the sheepfold. Pastors are content and happy when tending the needs of their flock. They tend to be people-minded and carry a deep concern for the well-being of those to whom they are ministering.

Prophets will most often work with Apostles and Pastors in the local church. Apostles understand and appreciate the prophetic ministry. Most of them carry a portion of prophetic ministry and love to work alongside of Prophets. The prophetic is a bold anointing. That's why the apostolic gets along so well with the prophetic; they both have bold flavor on their lives! Prophets and Pastors typically have extreme opposite personalities, vision and flow. These differences can easily be a catalyst for conflict in the absence of good training.

As we have already established, the gift of prophecy is given to the Church to build, comfort and exhort (1 Corinthians 14:3). This means that all believers may at times function in a measure of prophecy. That measure can be for their private lives (personal direction and understanding) or for a public gathering. In fact, the Church should welcome the prophetic ministry and hunger for its operation!

Pray without ceasing. In every thing give thanks: for this is the will of God in Christ Jesus concerning you. Quench not the Spirit. Despise not prophesyings. (1 Thessalonians 5:17-20)

Wherefore, brethren, covet to prophesy, and forbid not to speak with tongues. (1 Corinthians 14:39)

The instruction to the Church is to embrace and establish prophetic ministry in its midst by inviting the gift of prophecy to flow in our gatherings. Ask God to open the eyes of the people as the Apostle Paul did (Ephesians 1) and earnestly seek revelation from heaven.

A Church with a Vibrant Prophetic Ministry is:

- One where the river of God is flowing.

God is our refuge and strength, a very present help in trouble. Therefore will not we fear, though the earth be removed, and though the mountains be carried into the midst of the sea;Though the waters thereof roar and be troubled, though the mountains shake with the swelling thereof. Selah. There is a river, the streams whereof shall make glad the city of God, the holy place of the tabernacles of the most High. God is in the midst of her; she shall not be moved: God shall help her, and that right early. (Psalm. 46:1-5)

And he shall be like a tree planted by the rivers of water, that bringeth forth his fruit in his season; his leaf also shall not wither; and whatsoever he doeth shall prosper. (Psalm 1:3)

In that day sing ye unto her, A vineyard of red wine. I the Lord do keep it; I will water it every moment: lest any hurt it, I will keep it night and day. (Isaiah 27:2-3)

- One that recognizes the need for prophetic ministry.

This is the beginning of cultivating a prophetic atmosphere in a local church. The leaders must see the need for Spirit leading and development.

- One where spiritual sight is released, destinies established and people advancing.

A prophetic church is one where spiritual insight, vision and destiny is released.

Surely the Lord God will do nothing, but he revealeth his secret unto his servants the prophets. (Amos 3:7)

- One that builds and moves by faith.
- One dimension of the prophetic anointing is that it is a building anointing. By releasing insight, it sparks faith for building!

In the Bible one of the Greek words used when referring to the word of God is *rhema* which means *spoken word*. When there is a spoken word of God released it contains faith! Faith is the result of revelation. As God speaks, vision is released. Faith is the spirit of seeing and saying:

We having the same spirit of faith, according as it is written, I believed, and therefore have I spoken; we also believe, and therefore speak. (2 Corinthians 4:13)

- One that embraces the moving of the gifts of the Spirit.

In a church with a prophetic atmosphere there is a hunger for the gifts of the Spirit.

- One that brings government and order to the flow of the Spirit without quenching it.

Let the prophets speak two or three, and let the other judge. If any thing be revealed to another that sitteth by, let the first hold his peace. For ye may all prophesy one by one, that all may learn, and all may be comforted. And the spirits of the prophets are subject to the prophets. For God is not the author of confusion, but of peace, as in all churches of the saints. (1 Cor. 14:29-33)

Wherefore, brethren, covet to prophesy, and forbid not to speak with tongues. Let all things be done decently and in order. (1 Cor. 14:39-40-)

The call of the five-fold gift of Prophet is one that is established before a person is ever born *(Jeremiah 1:5)*. No amount of training, mentoring or impartation can create Prophets. What these things can do is to properly train believers to function in a greater level of prophetic ministry. Training can also identify a prophetic gift inside of a person and help bring that gift forward. There may be a Prophet who is unsure of their calling and through training they identify the call and begin to run with it. I would guarantee that a true Prophet has already been having many prophetic encounters throughout their life because the gift and call were always there.

A lot of the trouble that takes place in the local church concerning prophetic ministry happens as the lines are blurred between believers functioning in a dimension of prophetic ministry and the calling of a Prophet. However, through teaching and training these errors can be avoided.

All of the five-fold ministry gifts are called not only to do but also to equip. For example, while the Evangelist will preach, get souls saved and move in miracles, they are also called to equip the Body of Christ to evangelize. This is the true New Testament pattern of the Church.

And he gave some, apostles; and some, prophets; and some, evangelists; and some, pastors and teachers; For the perfecting of the saints, for the work of the ministry, for the edifying of the body of Christ. (Ephesians 4:11-12)

We have already established that in addition to dreams, prophetic words, healing ministry and other gifts, the Prophet must also have a teaching or preaching ministry. Prophets typically come into a region and pick up on both the plan of God for that region and the hindrances that exist within the region.

Then the Lord put forth his hand, and touched my mouth. And the Lord said unto me, Behold, I have put my words in thy mouth. See, I have this day set thee over the nations and over the kingdoms, to root out, and to pull down, and to destroy, and to throw down, to build, and to plant. (Jeremiah 1:9-10)

Prophetic insight empowers rooting out, pulling down and destroying the plans of the enemy. The Prophet sees into the spirit realm and identifies the tricks of the devil that are trying to oppose God's plan in a region. Identifying the spiritual foes in a territory is part of the work of transformation.

Not only will the Prophet minister insight to the region but very often they will give one-on-one prophetic ministry to people in meetings. There is something very powerful that happens when a Prophet speaks and declares destiny over the lives of the people of God. I have seen that when one-on-one prophetic ministry is flowing, people tend to flock to the meetings. However, this is not the only facet of the Prophet's ministry. Most of the time, the primary hunger of people toward the prophetic ministry is the pursuit of a personal word. They long for someone to "read their mail."

The Prophet is like the other five-fold gifts, they are called to be *Equippers.* Equipping means teaching, training, imparting and activating. One thing that a Prophet absolutely cannot do is create other Prophets. An individual either has that gift on his or her life or they do not. Prophetic seminars, conferences and schools should have a profound impact upon all those who attend by increasing their knowledge and imparting to them. There is a desperate need for healthy training concerning the prophetic ministry. One of the errors with prophetic schools and seminars is creating a culture where the bar is set at the Prophet's office thus elevating prophetic believers into a gift that they are not called to.

A Prophet absolutely can and should equip the Church to be more prophetic. Prophetic equipping should increase hunger for Spirit leading and the flow of prophetic ministry in people's lives. Actually when people become equipped they transition from continually seeking a word from someone else to becoming a prophetic person who is hearing from God on their own behalf. Then when that person receives a prophetic word it confirms what they have already been hearing.

A church with a well-equipped prophetic ministry is one in which the people become prophetic. Again, this does not mean that they are all Prophets.

CHAPTER 7

Developing a Prophetic Culture in a Church

n this chapter, we will discuss several keys to developing a prophetic culture in the local church.

1. Seeing the five-fold as equippers and not just doers.

Each ministry gift imparts a measure of Christ's ministry into the lives of the people, creating a fully functioning and mature Bride.

2. Creating an atmosphere of passionate worship, intense prayer and hunger.

Atmospheres give birth to experiences. When a ministry intentionally builds an atmosphere filled with God's presence and real hunger, miracles flow freely. Prophetic ministry is one that is very aware of atmospheres. It is key to create a culture of hunger. The worship ministry plays a vital role in establishing a prophetic atmosphere. There absolutely must be radical worship that goes after the heart of God and is unafraid to prophesy in music! There is a new breed of Davidic worship leaders arising in this hour who will be on the **frontlines** of God's move!

David led Israel into a great time of prosperity and victory as he established unending worship in the Kingdom. He not only approved of it, he participated in it wholeheartedly. Worship leaders cannot just sing the newest song with perfect pitch and expect their talent to release the presence of God. They must be willing to totally abandon themselves and get lost in His presence so that the people will follow. Prayer, worship and hunger are key to creating the right atmosphere.

Releasing the song of the Lord is a key component to creating a prophetic atmosphere in a church or ministry! The song of the Lord is the spontaneous release of prophetic utterance in music. At times it can be releasing God's heart over the people and other times it is releasing a fresh prophetic anthem of worship unto God.

> *Then Hezekiah gave the order to offer the burnt offering on the altar. When the burnt offering began, the song to the Lord also began with the trumpets, accompanied by the instruments of David, king of Israel. (2 Chronicles 29:27)*

> *All these were under the direction of their father to sing in the house of the Lord, with cymbals, harps and lyres, for the service of the house of God. Asaph, Jeduthun and Heman were under the direction of the king. Their number who were trained in singing*

to the Lord, with their relatives, all who were skillful, was 288. (1 Chronicles 25:6-7)

3. Releasing the flow of the streams of God.

On the inside of every Spirit-filled believer are powerful rivers. Many Christians live their entire lives never discovering or releasing the rivers of healing on the inside of them, the rivers of joy, the rivers of revelation or the rivers of love. In the great commission *(Mark 16:15-18)*, every believer was sent forth with supernatural power! That was not just for ministers but for Christians. A prophetic atmosphere has the potential to release those rivers and help believers step into a deeper realm.

Now on the last day, the great day of the feast, Jesus stood and cried out, saying, "If anyone is thirsty, let him come to Me and drink. He who believes in Me, as the Scripture said, 'From his innermost being will flow rivers of living water.'" But this He spoke of the Spirit, whom those who believed in Him were to receive; for the Spirit was not yet given, because Jesus was not yet glorified. (John 7:37-39)

4. Creating a platform for prophetic mentoring.

Much of the confusion in the local church concerning the prophetic has come in the absence of mentoring. As Elijah was nearing the completion of his ministry, the Lord spoke to him to go and find his successor. That was a difficult task! It takes a person who is humble and free from insecurity to appoint and train their successor. I think there is a powerful paradigm revealed in this story. Seasoned Prophets should be raising up prophetic sons and daughters with the full intent that their ministries receive a double portion and succeed beyond that of their mentor's ministry.

> **And the Lord said unto him, Go, return on thy way to the wilderness of Damascus: and when thou comest, anoint Hazael to be king over Syria: And Jehu the son of Nimshi shalt thou anoint to be king over Israel: and Elisha the son of Shaphat of Abel–meholah shalt thou anoint to be prophet in thy room. So he departed thence, and found Elisha the son of Shaphat, who was plowing with twelve yoke of oxen before him, and he with the twelfth: and Elijah passed by him, and cast his mantle upon him. (1 Kings 19:15-16, 19)**

Elijah mentored Elisha as they traveled together doing the work of the ministry. When the appointed time came for Elijah to depart, Elisha asked for a double portion.

> **And it came to pass, when they were gone over, that Elijah said unto Elisha, Ask what I shall do for thee, before I be taken away from thee. And Elisha said, I pray thee, let a double portion of thy spirit be upon me. And he said, Thou hast asked a hard thing: nevertheless, if thou see me when I am taken from thee, it shall be so unto thee; but if not, it shall not be so. (2 Kings 2:9-10)**

The amount of anointing was not a hard thing! It was the commitment on the part of Elisha. He was asking for a sonship inheritance blessing. In the custom of Israel the eldest son received a double portion inheritance (Deuteronomy 21:17). A son is unlike a student or co-worker; a son is with the father and is faithful to the family until the end. That was the hard thing! Elisha had to **complete the journey** with his mentor in order to get the double portion.

In *Luke 28:18-20*, Jesus told His followers to go into all the earth and **make disciples!** Disciples are not just hearers, they are followers. Disciples must be trained, equipped and taught. We create disciples by leading through example, not just explaining but demonstrating and then allowing them to try.

5. Giving grace to those who miss it.

As prophetic believers are mentored and trained, they will make mistakes. A training atmosphere needs to be one that is soaked in grace and forgiveness. When someone is new to the gifts of the Spirit they may minister in a way that is not the most wise. They need guidance and instruction to sharpen the gift. Prophetic mentoring should really be about identifying and sharpening gifts.

6. Establishing protocol.

This is really key in a church or ministry with a strong prophetic culture. The leaders need to seek God and establish expectations in line with the word. What is the order of the house? If someone has a prophetic word in a corporate gathering, what is the preferred way to deliver it? Remember you must communicate and then communicate again the principles over and over. In many churches only sixty percent of the members are there in a main service and often people either don't understand or forget. Repetitive communication of vision is a must!

Are there prophetic teams? If so, what is the expectation of team members and how do you join? Are there classes? When and where? What is the policy for one-on-one prophetic ministry? Is there an appointed prayer team for altar time? I have found that answering these questions and clearly communicating those answers is vital. Sons and daughters will gladly receive the input and honor the culture of the house. Rebels will not!

7. Dealing with renegade spirits.

It is an unfortunate reality that a ministry which demonstrates Spirit-filled life and establishes prophetic ministry will have to deal with problematic individuals. In my mind there are distinctions between those who cause problems:

- Some are new and simply don't know any better. These people are the ones who break protocol and do something that is not in line with the order of the house but their intent is not harmful. The best approach is to share with them what is expected and provide some loving correction.
- Others are rebellious and choose not to honor. They may even have a theology that rejects the principle of submission to authority. This is a dangerous situation because these individuals will actually use their gift to sow dissension and create confusion. You must enforce the order of the house with strength when dealing with this. Most of the time, they will not stay where there is strong leadership. A wrong theology that refuses to recognize or honor God-ordained leadership can easily embrace an Absalom spirit *(2 Samuel chapters 13-18)* and create a church split.

- Some are actually being used by false spirits to create havoc. Prophetic ministry will be opposed by wrong spirits. One of the chief spirits that attempts to infiltrate prophetic ministry is the Jezebel spirit. Jezebel competes with and hates an authentic prophetic anointing. A Jezebel spirit will identify itself as a Prophet. They are not recognized by any valid leader nor do they have the character to back up the claim, they are self-appointed *(Revelation 2:20)*. A spirit of Jezebel will come in with many claims and appearing to be a real answer to prayer but the motive is wrong! The spirit establishes itself as a spiritual leader in the lives of immature believers and boasts of its spirituality. It will undermine leadership and create a great division. The person with the spirit must be set free, which requires recognition and true repentance on their part. If they are unwilling to repent and get free then they must leave or they will cause greater destruction. There will be other spirits that are drawn to a place with strong prophetic ministry and those in charge must be watchful and use wisdom. It is common to attract people carrying some "false fire" or wrong spiritual influences. This is why the prophetic ministry must include teaching! Without teaching, people cannot learn or become free.

The opportunity to lead (rather than exercise a gift) in a local church or ministry should be granted according to character not gifting. A strong ministry must create a culture of honor and family. In order to be healthy, there are boundaries and expectations mixed with lots of love and grace.

Renegades are unteachable and unwilling to become a part of a healthy spiritual family. They thrive on walking alone and are drawn to prophetic ministry because they wrongly believe that it validates their rebellion. A person carrying a renegade spirit does not have fruit of longevity nor can they point to anyone that they have had long-term spiritual relationship with as a spiritual father or mother in their life. You can quickly identify a renegade by their lack of fruit. Satan lusted for power. Witchcraft is a seduction that is carried out by offering access to spiritual power. We must be very mindful of those who desire power without loyalty, servanthood or character.

> **Lay hands suddenly on no man, neither be partaker of other men's sins: keep thyself pure. (1 Timothy 5:22)**

This instruction was given by Paul to Timothy in regards to appointing leaders. Our approval of leaders is a holy thing and not to be taken lightly.

> **Now I beseech you, brethren, mark them which cause divisions and offences contrary to the doctrine which ye have learned; and avoid them. For they that are such serve not our Lord Jesus Christ, but their own belly; and by good words and fair speeches deceive the hearts of the simple. (Romans 16:17-18)**

Sometimes you have to cut off the voice and influence of a renegade spirit. It is very difficult for certain people to handle conflict but it is a part of leadership. People who create division should not be given influence in a ministry.

CHAPTER 8

Judging and Stewarding Personal Prophecy

F irst of all, we must make a bit of a distinction between the prophetic office of the Old Testament versus the New Testament. The primary change is the condition of man. Under the Old Testament, man was separated from God and void of inward leading. The primary way that God communicated with people was through outward signs and words. Prophets served as direct mouthpieces, going to God on behalf of the people.

Under the New Testament, Christians have been born-again with a spirit man that has full access to the Father. God is no longer communicating with mankind primarily through outward signs or manifestations but through inward leading. The greatest leading in the life of a believer who is following God should be the leading of the Holy Spirit taking place in the inside of them. The Holy Spirit leads through: the inner witness, thought-like revelations, leading of peace, hearing the still small voice, visions and inner visions, open visions and night visions. God communicates in many ways. Our job is to listen and heed His leading!

Prophets are now given as gifts to Jesus' Bride (*Ephesians 4*). All five of the ministry gifts are given as gifts of grace to minister, equip and build up the Body. Prophets may very well speak things into the life of a believer that opens their eyes and shifts their life! Yet, the believer is no longer solely reliant on seeking a Prophet to hear from God. Nor should a believer base their entire life on the revelation of another person.

The vast majority of personal prophetic words should be confirming words that agree with what a Christian has heard in their private time with God. If someone gives you a word that you are to sell everything you own and move to a foreign land, if this is not something that you have received from God, put it on the shelf and *do not just run with it!*

There are some times when a personal prophecy may not be a confirming word:

- If a person is not really seeking God and spending quality time with Him, then a prophetic word may speak to some things that they have not received due to their lack of fellowship.
- If there is wickedness or sin in a person's life, a Prophet may expose it. That is one of the difficult tasks given to the prophetic office. Prophets are used to expose things that are demonic and destructive in the lives of people and ministries. This is not an excuse for a believer to go around blasting people. This is something that comes with the governing authority of a Prophet.

- If a person has left their relationship with God and has not heard His voice in a long time.

Keys to judging a personal directional prophecy.

The first question is, who gave it to you and how was it delivered? Why is this important? Many times a wrong word is evidenced by the way that it is delivered. I have seen many "parking lot prophets" that roam from church to church and engage in a renegade prophetic ministry that operates outside of any blessing from the house and creates conflict by speaking to the ambitions of people instead of pure prophetic declaration.

And we beseech you, brethren, to know them which labour among you, and are over you in the Lord, and admonish you. (1 Thessalonians 5:12)

You should have some type of knowledge of a person's character before allowing them to speak into your life. A person who claims to be a Prophet but disrespects order and tears down more than they ever build up is indeed deceived. The problem that arises is that sometimes a deceived person still has an accurate gift that will draw people to them. How can this be? There are two answers:

1. The gifts and calling of God are without repentance *(Romans 11:29)*. Simply put, God doesn't remove a gift because a person gets in error. It is quite possible for someone to speak out a prophecy with accuracy but have poor fruit. The other important thing to know here is that the highest level of prophetic operation is not

just revealing the desires of a human heart, but releasing the heart of the Father and revealing the end of the matter! Many times, personal prophecy contains a dimension of rebuke as well in order to align the person with God's heart and plan for them.

2. There is a false spirit in operation. There are many people out there who have opened themselves up to wrong spirits and they have communication in the spirit realm with demonic spirits. They can give accurate information but cannot release the Father's heart because they are blocked by their deception. On more than one occasion I have seen a spirit of divination operating through someone and mimicking the prophetic but the end result is destruction. This is why knowing the fruit and doing things in order is important.

Judge all prophecies by the written word of God.

We have also a more sure word of prophecy; whereunto ye do well that ye take heed, as unto a light that shineth in a dark place, until the day dawn, and the day star arise in your hearts. (2 Peter 1:9)

And I fell at his feet to worship him. And he said unto me, See thou do it not: I am thy fellowservant, and of thy brethren that have the testimony of Jesus: worship God: for the testimony of Jesus is the spirit of prophecy. (Revelation 19:10)

In the beginning was the Word, and the Word was with God, and the Word was God. (John 1:1)

No prophetic word should disagree with the written word of God. In fact, the Church should actively examine prophetic utterances to make sure that they are in line with God's word and boldly toss out any that are not. For example, if a person prophesies that a married person is to leave their spouse and marry someone else, this is blatant deception and witchcraft at work. If a renegade tries to prophesy to a church member that God wants them to rebel against the leaders, again, that is deception and a false spirit. Never accept a prophetic word that cannot be properly judged by God's word.

Ask yourself if the word confirms what you have been led to do. If God clearly directed a person to have a business that would be fruitful and be a place of ministry for them, then they received a prophetic word to sell the business and start a church, they should never act on that word. If it does not bear witness in the inner man, then either put it on the shelf as it could be for a future time or throw it out altogether.

When receiving a directional word get *wise* counsel. Take the word to trusted advisers and ask what they think of it.

For by wise counsel thou shalt make thy war: and in multitude of counsellors there is safety. (Proverbs 24:6)

When judging a personal prophecy, honor your spiritual relationships and seek their input. If your parents are godly people ask them what they think. If you are married and your spouse is serving the Lord, seek their input. The people who know you best and are committed to God's will for you can often see things that you may not see. Also, seek the input of your spiritual leadership. Go to your Pastor or apostolic leadership and ask for insight. So many times I have seen a prophecy steer someone in the wrong direction and their lack of communication with godly leaders empowered the deception.

A number of years ago, a guest speaker came to a church that I was leading and ministered to a precious young lady in the prayer line. The minister spoke some words that were unclear and created confusion. I believe that the intent of the minister was good but the word was not on target. Over the next few weeks a blanket of confusion came upon the young lady. As I was ministering one day in the church, the Lord spoke clearly for me to pray for her and break the words and also break confusion. When I did that, it completely lifted and peace settled in on her.

Avoiding error in prophetic ministry in the local church

As we have discussed throughout this writing, the prophetic ministry is a valuable tool in the local church when properly established and governed. There are challenges that come with prophetic ministry but the reward far outweighs the challenges.

One of the first truths that must be embraced and understood is that there are different parameters and functions of prophetic believers versus the office of the Prophet.

A New Testament Prophet is foundational to the health and life of the global Church *(Ephesians 2:20)*. The Prophet carries a revelatory gift that is unparalleled. He or she speaks the very depths of the heart of God and carries a deep passion for His presence.

Prophets are endued with a governing anointing. They are referenced in the New Testament as working alongside of

Apostles and Teachers to build and guide the Church. There is a grace upon their lives to release directional words and revelation into the Church in submission to the authority and government of the house.

> **Now there were in the church that was at Antioch certain prophets and teachers; as Barnabas, and Simeon that was called Niger, and Lucius of Cyrene, and Manaen, which had been brought up with Herod the tetrarch, and Saul. As they ministered to the Lord, and fasted, the Holy Ghost said, Separate me Barnabas and Saul for the work whereunto I have called them. And when they had fasted and prayed, and laid their hands on them, they sent them away. So they, being sent forth by the Holy Ghost, departed unto Seleucia; and from thence they sailed to Cyprus. (Acts 13:1-4)**

When a traveling Prophet comes into the local church they are operating under the authority of the Pastor, Apostle or Senior Leader(s). A seasoned Prophet will understand and respect this principle. The only exception would be a situation where there is severe evil and deception, in which case a Prophet would most likely depart.

> **And we beseech you, brethren, to know them which labour among you, and are over you in the Lord, and admonish you; And to esteem them very highly in love for their work's sake. And be at peace among yourselves. (1 Thessalonians 5:12-13)**

God has entrusted the care of the flock to the leadership that He has placed in the house. The local leadership is the final authority of that house. Of course, they may and should have someone that is in apostolic oversight of them. My point is this: that a visiting prophetic ministry must submit their gift to the set leadership of the house regardless of the size or scope of their ministry. This does not mean that they water down their message or compromise their flow but actually the intensity of the flow should increase if the leaders are honorable and hungry.

There must be an understanding of the role of prophetic believers *(not those walking in the five-fold gift of Prophet)* in the Church. Prophetic believers must operate under the authority of the house and so their words should be submitted under the leader in an open and honest manner for examination and confirmation.

Prophetic believers have unlimited access to the realm of the Spirit and may easily pick up on many things concerning the local church. They must realize though that they have not been given authority by God or grace upon their gifting to provide spiritual government.

I remember a number of years ago I went to preach at a church and met some of the prayer team. They asked to speak with me after the meeting was over. They showed me a bulletin board that hung in the church where very specific directional prophecies were pinned. One of the prophetic words that they gave was that the church was going to relocate to a particular place by an exact date. That day came and went with no results. They asked me what I thought about this. I immediately felt grieved. I told them that I thought they were trying to govern the vision of the house and that they were getting "out there." The Pastor needed to be establishing the vision and leading the major changes. They could certainly take what they picked up on in prayer and submit it to him but they were operating outside of their authority.

Prophetic believers should honor the culture and expectations of the ministry that they are a part of. Most places that recognize prophetic ministry amongst believers set some guidelines. For example, if you get a word, what is the proper way of sharing that? Rather than just demand the right to deliver it, work alongside of the leadership team to steward the word and release it in the most effective manner.

Do not entertain a spirit of offense if someone asks you to hold a word or release it in a particular time. Also, do not let an accusing spirit operate through you by railing on a leader who does their job in establishing godly order and protecting the sheep. I can tell you from my own experience pastoring local churches that some very odd people come through the doors and want to pray for people and prophesy over them. The Bible is clear that we will give an account for our stewardship over ministries and it is our job to create a healthy, Spirit-led atmosphere that is a safe place.

I had a young lady that came to my church a number of years ago who had come out of a background with some occult activity. She was delivered and set free in our ministry. One day an older man showed up at the church and began to regularly attend services. I had a real check in my spirit and I noticed he would wear odd trinkets and jewelry that felt unclean to me.

Later on, the young lady came to me and told me that he always pursued her and talked to her. He had patted her shoulder or made some type of fairly innocent physical contact with her numerous times. She began to have demonic encounters like the ones she had before being delivered. I knew that they were tied to that man.

You never know who it is that may want to pray for you or speak over you! That is why healthy boundaries are established; they are there for protection, not to quench God's Spirit. We prayed and took action. We discerned a false occult spirit on that man. Eventually he left and the young lady was fine.

Let the prophets speak two or three, and let the other judge. (1 Corinthians 14:29)

Prophecies given in the local church by prophetic believers should be given openly and welcome judgment or insight from other leaders. It is always a bad sign to me when people refuse to share their prophetic words with leaders. This type of secrecy can fuel rebellion and deception.

Prophetic believers should avoid giving detailed directional prophecies to people in the church without direction or permission from the senior leaders. There are a couple of things to note here. One is that a believer flowing in the simple gift of prophecy may pick up on something about a person's future but their primary mission is to edify, exhort and comfort rather than direct. It is very easy to get a leading and then prophesy it in such a way that it leads to a problem.

For example: let's say a prophetic person attending a church really notices a spirit of worship on someone, they go to that person and release a word that they are called to lead the worship team. That word can create a tremendous amount of confusion. The person who gave the word does not have the authority to establish leaders in that house but they are prophesying leadership positions. The person who receives the word may take it in and grow weary and frustrated when they are not asked to lead worship. Now, that word could have been given in a more healthy way. The believer could just tell the person that they see a real passion for worship on their life and exhort them. That opens up a hunger for them to pursue God and find their place without creating confusion or attempting to govern.

Directional prophecies are not something that is going to be a constant flow outside of the office of the Prophet. Believers will pick up on things here and there but not at the depth of the Prophet. It is best for prophetic believers to avoid detailed directional prophecies in the local church unless they are released and authorized to do so by their leaders.

There are many depths to the prophetic flow that can and will unfold for the believer who has a prophetic spirit. There are words of knowledge, healings (emotional and physical), deliverances, powerful one-on-one ministry and much more.

Secondly, Prophets can be emotional by nature and struggle with the trap of negativity. Remember when Elijah was in the cave ready to quit just after his greatest victory? Prophetic people can easily fall into a lifestyle of perceiving the glass is half empty. This is partially because of how they are wired. They perceive and sense at a heightened level. Much of the Prophet's ministry is calling the people of God up higher.

The Apostle Paul demonstrated his love for the churches that he helped establish and the depth of relationship with his spiritual sons and daughters. He often corrected false doctrine and even identified people with destructive motives within the churches that he governed. He DID NOT go around blasting and correcting leaders, people or churches with which he had no relationship or investment.

There are many inexperienced prophetic voices that spend a considerable amount of their time rebuking and correcting ministries and believers that they have never had relationship with or invested into. This is extremely unfruitful and unwise. Fathers bring correction through relationship and earned respect. They sow into those with whom they have labored intensely and who are under their spiritual care.

Correction can be one of the greatest catalysts for growth in the life of a believer and in a ministry if it is received properly. There is **no** precedence for ministers or believers continually criticizing and correcting ministries where they have no spiritual relationship or authority. I think it is often the fruit of a religious spirit that is puffed up in pride. True humility longs to see the Body come into destiny and does not take pleasure in correction but provides it through proper relationship.

> *I write not these things to shame you, but as my beloved sons I warn you. For though ye have ten thousand instructors in Christ, yet have ye not many fathers: for in Christ Jesus I have begotten you through the gospel. (1 Corinthians 4:14-15)*

Prophetic Assignments

The prophetic office and ministry is multi-faceted. There are many dimensions of the prophetic ministry. Let's examine some of the flows of the prophetic. One of the unique prophetic dimensions is that of *The Seer.*

Now the acts of David the king, first and last, behold, they are written in the book of Samuel the seer, and in the book of Nathan the prophet, and in the book of Gad the seer. (1 Chronicles 29:29)

In the Old Testament, one of the Hebrew words used for Prophet is the word *roeh* which means to see or perceive. This describes a Prophet whose primary source of revelation is vision, dreams and sight related experiences. This is someone who has frequent interruptions with natural sight as they look into the realm of the spirit. This is also a function of prophetic anointing that can be activated in the life of a believer who is not necessarily a prophet but receives most of their revelation in a visual form.

Another Hebrew word used in the Old Testament for Prophet is *nabi.* This literally means to bubble up. This indicates a Prophet who hears and releases what they hear! They may not receive as many visions as the Seer but they receive powerful utterances from the mouth of God that erupt in their spirit. This is one who *hears and declares.* Again, there are prophetic believers who receive most of their insight from the voice of the Lord rather than through vision.

The third word used in the Old Testament for Prophet is the Hebrew word *hoseh* which also means to see or perceive. This word is used in relationship to Prophets, advisors to kings and also associated with musicians.

Types of Prophetic Assignments:

- **The Seer**- As described above, a Prophet with frequent and uncommon visions, they continually look into the dimension of the unseen spirit realm and release revelation from the visions.
- **The Dreamer**- Connected to the seer function. Experiencing frequent and significant prophetic dreams.
- **The Psalmist**- A musical Prophet or a worship minster with a heavy prophetic anointing.

And it came to pass, when the evil spirit from God was upon Saul, that David took an harp, and played with his hand: so Saul was refreshed, and was well, and the evil spirit departed from him. (1 Samuel 16:23)

David was first and foremost a worshipper. He had a strong prophetic call that was divinely linked with music. There are those called into prophetic music ministry that will release sounds and songs, opening up the atmosphere and breaking through the darkness.

- **The Minstrel**- A prophetic musician.

But now bring me a minstrel. And it came to pass, when the minstrel played, that the hand of the Lord came upon him. (2 Kings 3:15)

- **The Scribe Prophet**- A writer who will receive and release the word of the Lord through writing.
- **Power Prophets**- Those who carry an unusual dimension of demonstration and power!

And it came to pass, as they were burying a man, that, behold, they spied a band of men; and they cast the man into the sepulchre of Elisha: and when the man was let down, and touched the bones of Elisha, he revived, and stood up on his feet. (2 Kings 13:21)

There was so much power stored up in the bones of Elisha that it brought the dead back to life! There are people who function in the prophetic and carry a real power anointing.

- **Local and Regional Prophets**- People called to be a part of a five-fold team functioning primarily within a ministry or region. Their dominant voice will be within a particular area.
- **Global Prophetic Ministry**- Jeremiah was called to speak to nations!

See, I have this day set thee over the <u>nations</u> and over the kingdoms, to root out, and to pull down, and to destroy, and to throw down, to build, and to plant. (Jeremiah 1:10)

This level of prophetic ministry carries a different dimension of authority and insight. A global Prophet is granted a platform to release words over nations and territories. They will come in direct conflict with spiritual rulers in the nations that they prophesy over. They will have uncommon favor with govern-mental and business leaders in nations. This is the favor that is upon their calling. Global Prophets will often have media ministries in order to deliver the words that God gives them. They are people who speak to current events, coming crisis and blessing, leaders on a broad scale, political structures, elections and officials.

- **Media Mandates**- There are both apostolic and pro-phetic leaders whose primary function will be in media. They are called to create and birth media that captures and releases the word of the Lord.
- **Prophetic Artists**- People who create from a place of prophetic expression. They create that which they have heard or seen.
- **Prayer Mantles**- Because Prophets are friends of God, there are many prophetic leaders who will pioneer and lead prayer, worship and intercession ministries. They carry the spirit of burning and live to unite the Bride with her Beloved.

My attempt here is to shed a little light on the wide variety of prophetic assignments and mantles. In no way is this work a complete description. Prophets are radical seekers who think and live outside of the box. There are multitudes of expres-sions that I have failed to list but I hope these descriptions pro-vide some insight.

Conclusion

And they rose early in the morning, and went forth into the wilderness of Tekoa: and as they went forth, Jehoshaphat stood and said, Hear me, O Judah, and ye inhabitants of Jerusalem; Believe in the Lord your God, so shall ye be established; believe his prophets, so shall ye prosper. (2 Chronicles 20:20)

The prophetic ministry is an invitation to step into a higher realm of insight, strength and blessing. When prophetic words are released, they are saturated with strength and life. God has not hidden His heart from us at all. In fact, He has invited us on a marvelous journey to discover the vast wonder of His unfailing love for us.

At the purest of prophetic ministry is the revealing of the Father's good plans and instruction for His people. The Church of this hour needs the prophetic ministry. There are multitudes of people who desperately need the direction that comes through healthy prophetic anointing.

He that receiveth a prophet in the name of a prophet shall receive a prophet's reward; and he that receiveth a righteous man in the name of a righteous man shall receive a righteous man's reward. (Matthew 10:41)

Just as the barren Shunammite woman received a powerful miracle so can God's people receive miracles and divine elevation from the ministry of Prophets. I thank God that He is still raising up Seers in this hour who have seen the plans of the Lord and declare them to His people. As the people of God welcome prophetic ministry and receive from it there is great reward.

We desperately need all the gifts and callings of God alive and active in today's Church. God never intended His Kingdom to be a one man show! It is all about loving, investing, training and activating. There is no call that is a little call! Everything that the Lord asks His people to do is important.

I firmly believe that the prophetic ministry is another vital link in the chain but *every link* is important. My prayer is that you find your place and function in the unction for your life! Prophets are bold fiery leaders who live in the realm of hearing, knowing and seeing. They are uncommon people who hold precious anointing to share with God's children.

I want to see the Church build strong healthy ministries that usher in Revival and Awakening. I am convinced that the prophetic voice is key to the **Emerging Move of God**. The Prophets are needed to help build the powerful places of transformation that are arising in this hour. Prophetic words will fuel the plans of the Apostles and link the people together to dig the deep wells of Revival.

Let's push, pray, contend and love on Jesus as we pursue all that He has for us. May your spirit be strong, your heart at peace and your spirit eyes wide open. Let's **release the prophetic** and gather the harvest.

About the Author

Ryan LeStrange is the founder and leader of Impact International Ministries, headquartered in Bristol, Virginia. Impact is an apostolic-based ministry that has birthed several local churches in Southwest Virginia with a vision to circle the globe with the Fire of Revival. Ryan has a burning desire for media ministry in that he has co-founded **AwakeningTV.com**, a media outlet created to host revival inspired services, featuring ministers and messages both past and present.

Ryan has been preaching the gospel for more than half of his life. As a young man, he trained at the Bible college of his spiritual father, Dr. Norvel Hayes. His time with Dr. Hayes developed in him a passion for the ministry of healing, the operation of faith, flowing in the Gifts of the Spirit and a longing for a move of the glory of God.

As a modern-day Revivalist, Ryan moves strongly in the power of God, traveling the globe to ignite Revival Fires. He is one of the senior leaders of New Breed Revival Network, a network of ministers committed to seeing revival birthed in America and the nations of the world.

Ryan's desire is to see God's people and the Church rise up to their full potential and operate under the ordination of heaven. All that he does, he does with the mandate he received from God at age seventeen to, "Take My power to the nations of the earth."

He lives by the Scripture of Daniel 11:32.... "the people who know their God shall be strong and do great exploits."

Developing queens.com

Made in the USA
San Bernardino, CA
10 June 2017